# HARDEN NOT YOUR HEARTS ISRAEL

"Today, When You Hear His Voice"

Hebrew 3:7-8

Mitchell D. Ewing Sr.

# Harden Not Your Hearts Israel

"Today When You Hear His Voice"

Copyright© 2020 by Enlightenment Publishing, LLC

All rights reserved. No part of this publication may be reproduced, stored in a retrieval system, or transmitted in any form or by any means–electronic, mechanical, photocopying, recording, or otherwise–without the prior written permission of the Enlightenment Publishing, LLC, Surprise, Arizona 85374.

Scripture quotations taken from the Holy Bible, New Living Translation, copyright © 1996, 2004, 2007 by Tyndale House Foundation. Used by the permission

Scripture quotations taken from the Apocrypha ® Bible, Copyright © 1992, 1994, 1997, 2000, 2002, 2003 Used by permission." (www.Lockman.org)

Scripture quotations taken from the Hebrew-Greek Key Word Study King James Version® Bible by permission.

ISBN 978-0-9855490-5-3

Published By:


Enlightenment Publishing, LLC

Surprise, AZ 85374    EP

enlightpub@gmail.com                LLC

http://enlightpub.wix.com/enlightenment

**Promoting:**

**Consciousness * Conversation * Research**

# DEDICATION:

This book is being devoted to the entire nation of Awakened Hebrews: To my offspring who were scattered throughout the regions of Africa, as well as, the four corners of the world; inclusive of my brothers and sisters who are the direct descendants of the slave epidemic; more than ever, those children of the transatlantic slave trade scattered throughout the Americas.

# PREFACE

"In that day the root of Jesse, who shall stand as a signal for the peoples—of him shall the nations inquire, and his resting place shall be glorious.

In that day YAH will extend his hand yet a second time to recover the remnant that remains of his people, from Assyria, from Egypt, from Pathros, from Cush, from Elam, from Shinar, from Hamath, and from the coastlands or islands of the Mediterranean.

He will raise a signal for the nations and will assemble the **banished of Israel**; and gather the **dispersed or scattered of Judah** from the four corners of the earth."

Isaiah 11:10-12

# AUTHOR'S THOUGHTS

"This book is written to the True Children of Israel; the so-called "Blacks & Negroes": the various shades of brown: who has awakened in this truth but struggle with understanding their overall purpose, requirement, and direction from Abba Father.

At a time when there are so many doctrines (of devils) out there that are geared towards putting our people back into another form of bondage – that does more harm than good; that does more scattering us further apart then bringing us together; that focuses only on the external works of the flesh via ceremonial customs, practices, and celebrations, while simultaneously, ignoring the eternal works of righteousness & faith as commanded by our HaMashiach & reminded by the Ruach HaKodesh.

As in the days of our Messiah when many of his teachings were rejected; so too, will many discard these teachings because: <u>the servant is not above his master</u>. Furthermore, this book is not written to those who will disregard it; but to those who are striving to hear HIS VOICE: who will not harken unto the voice of another false deity.

## ACKNOWLEDGMENTS

My acknowledgments will continue as demonstrated in my previously writings and completed works. All thanks and praise to the Almighty YAH, our Creator and Abba Father, our Redeemer and Rescuer. Special thanks to my wife Bridget (Adiryah), my Hebrew queen – the true biblical description of a wife and mother:

"Her husband has full confidence in her and lacks nothing of value. She speaks with wisdom and faithful instruction is on her tongue. She watches over the affairs of her household and does not eat the bread of idleness. Her children arise and call her blessed; her husband also and he praises her."

And to our children who are dearly loved: Zaria, Zanetta, Zashanae, and Mitchell Jr. Continue to hear and heed the instructions of your father and embrace the nurturing of your mother and desire to learn and gain the clear understanding of your true Hebrew identity and heritage.

And to the rest of our Hebrew family residing all over the world – thank you for embracing us, loving us, and praying for us as we continue to grow together and share this truth to our people who are presently unaware of their precious birthright.

## TABLE OF CONTENTS

| | Introduction | 15 |
|---|---|---|
| 1 | The Mosaic & Eternal Law | 29 |
| 2 | The Rauch HaKadosh | 70 |
| 3 | Free But Yet Bound | 101 |
| 4 | Changing The Way We Think | 109 |
| 5 | A Prepared People For a Prepared Place | 131 |
| | About the Author | 159 |
| | Black Bible Character Images the Author | 161 |
| | References | 211 |

# INTRODUCTION

The awakening period has arrived and our eyes are finally opened to understanding. Our Hebrew ancestors (the so-called Negroes, the various shades of brown; human descendants according to the flesh, scattered throughout the four corners of the earth) are from a chosen generation, a royal priesthood, a set-apart Nation, a peculiar people who were called out of darkness (blinded by trickery and lies) into YAH's marvelous light (the ability to see clearly beyond the severe deceptions that have been programmed into the lives of our people for many generations). This is usually the extent of our awakening period for those whom the Most High has elected to know HIM (as Abba Father), as well as understanding who we are (as a Nation of people), and our role in the whole scheme of things, or the purpose of our existence for such a time as this.

And for all practical purposes and principles, the desired audience are those who are linked to biblical prophecy (according to various history books and writings, including the books of Deuteronomy 28 and Isaiah 11:11-13) – those whose ancestors are the immediate recipients of the vast number of **enslavements and oppressions** as early as Ancient Egypt, expanding through the period of the Judges and Kings (to included Edom), extending to Assyria, Babylon, Greece (Hellenization and Maccabean periods),

Rome, and continuing through the most recent and recognizable events of the Spanish Inquisition, the Arab slave trades, and the infamous Transatlantic slave trades, followed by Jim Crow, Apartheid (just to name a few) and the present human conditions of our people throughout the world.

With intense excitement and enthusiasm – we are overwhelmed with joy, and our hearts are full of praise; simultaneously, we become sorrowful and ashamed when we learn the reasons for our past and present captivities. In humility, we offer up solemn oaths of repentance through prayer to the MOST HIGH because he has graciously opened our eyes to understanding – for we have been awakened from a brutal deep sleep, once blinded but now granted access of truth through spiritual enlightenment as noted in the book of 2 Esdras 1: 35-37:

"...I will give to a people (the fallen house of Israel), which not having heard of me yet shall believe me; to whom I have showed no signs, yet they shall do what I commanded them. They have seen no prophets, yet they call their sins to remembrance and acknowledge them.

I take to witness the grace of the people to come, whose little ones rejoice in gladness: and though they have not seen me with bodily eyes (in the flesh), yet in spirit they believe the things that I say."

Without delay, our eagerness pushes us to share this eye-opening revelation with all those it pertains to: our fathers, our mothers, our spouses, our sons and daughters, our closest relatives, friends, neighbors, co-workers, and perhaps, our previous associations and affiliations: (i.e., church/religious organization members, sorority/fraternity brothers and sisters, so forth and etc.). But to no avail because we soon find out that those we expected to be the most excited are usually those who express little to no interest, and somehow think that you have lost your mind or joined a cult of some sort. Although this very important information is a life-changing experience (if applied appropriately) and essential to their well-being, it is stubbornly rejected.

Feeling alone and somewhat frustrated, attempting to comprehend why this good news became sour in the ears of those to whom it was appointed, we have to be reminded of what our Messiah expressed to those who accepted and declined his message:

**"…it is giving unto _YOU_ to know the mysteries of the Kingdom of Heaven, but to _THEM_ – it is not given."**

**"For this people's heart (Israel as a Nation) is waxed gross (or**

**hardened), and their ears are dull of hearing, and their eyes THEY have closed; lest at any time they should see with their eyes, and hear with their heart, and should be converted, and I should heal them." Matthew (Mattithyahu) 13:11; 15**

We, the children of our ancestors: Abraham (Avraham), Isaac (Yitschaq), and Jacob (Ya'aq0v) (the descendants of brown and black people (the so-called negroes) scattered throughout this present world as was prophesied) have been squashed and trodden down by the surrounding nations for so long that we don't desire to become a separate nation again but with a glimmer of a better hope. Only to be loved and accepted by those who constantly reject, neglect, and hate us. Conforming to modern standards and values of the nations in which we reside, we accept their religions, their gods and idols, their holidays and celebrations, their worldly achievements and philosophy, their political circus, their way of living and thinking, all of which are usually anchored in immoral principles and ethics.

This is why the Messiah expressed to his disciples regarding the current condition of a great people as was prophesied by Isaiah (Yesha'yahu) 6:9-10, as it is this day. This is also why the message of hope and salvation is unwanted and despised by children of Israel as it is this day, because we have been programmed to love and forgive our enemies (although they never seem to truly repent and change) and to hate ourselves (our own people with a callous heart). Representing our HaMaschiach (the

Messiah) is not loving our enemies (the surrounding nations), that's not what his writings tell us to do, or to forgive our enemies for hurting us as noted:

**"Don't you hear the uproar of your enemies? Don't you see that your arrogant enemies are rising up? They devise crafty schemes against your people; they conspire against your precious ones.**

**'Come," they say, 'let us wipe out Israel as a Nation. We will destroy the very memory or its/their existence. They (the surrounding nations that hates us and enslaved us) signed a treaty as allies against you.'" Psalm (Tehilliym) 83:2-5 (NLT)**

We have been lied to and taught in the Christian churches (all of our lives) that the passage in the Bible that says "love your enemies" means to love our slave masters/oppressors, including everyone that hurts us, and to hold them not guilty. But that is not what that passage was intended for and that is not its true meaning.

When the Messiah stated to "love your enemies" found in the Book of Matthew (Mattithyahu) 5:43-44, the biggest thing that we're never taught is to observe the living audience to whom he was speaking. His message was not intended for everyone in this passage, but to the Lost House of the Tribe of Israel only. Then the Messiah came back to clarify exactly who those enemies were. (He was asking his people to embrace and love):

"...Your enemies will be right in your own household!" Matthew (Mattithyahu) 10:36 (NLT)

Furthermore, the Messiah himself was quoting from the book of Micah (Miykah) 7:6 **regarding his people Israel**, which stated:

"For the son dishonors the father, the daughters rises up against her mother, the daughter-in-law against her mother-in-law; a man's enemies are the men of his own house."

Again:

"For the son despises his father. The daughter defies her mother. The daughter-in-law defies her mother-in-law. Your enemies are right in your own household! (NLT)

As we can observe, the Messiah was teaching the lost tribes of Israel how to **love the best and worst of their/our own PEOPLE** (not pertaining to loving and cuddling with those who have conspired against us as a Nation over many generations). But as you can see today (in this present age), we love everybody else except for our own people and treat each other poorly. And the reason why, even for those who have been enlightened in this spiritual awakening, is because many of us have not been **TRULY CONVERTED.**

"**Don't copy the world, but let YAH transform you into a new person by CHANGING THE WAY YOU THINK. Then you will learn to know YAH's will for you – which is good, pleasing, and perfect.**" Romans (Romaiym) 12: 2 (NLT)

"**And be not conformed to this world: but be ye transformed by the RENEWING of your MIND...**" Romans (Romaiym) 12: 2 (KJV)

> G165 - *aiōn*
> **Outline of Biblical Usage:**
> *I.* for ever, an unbroken age, perpetuity of eternity
> *II.* the worlds, universe
> *III.* period of time, age

The word "world" in this passage "aion" from the Greek transliteration (G165) means: the present age or period of time in which you live. So, if we were to reread the following and above passages and insert their true definition, they would read as such:

"Don't copy <u>the present age or period of time</u> in which you are currently residing in, but let YAH transform you into a new person by CHANGING THE WAY YOU THINK. Then you will learn to know YAH's will for you – which is good, pleasing, and perfect." Romans (Romaiym) 12:2 (NLT)

"<u>And be not conformed to this present age or period of time</u> in which you are currently residing in: but be ye transformed by the RENEWING of your MIND..." Romans (Romaiym) 12:2 (KJV)

This better understanding of the text holds extreme significance in accepting (presently) one of Israel's biggest struggles which is allowing YAH to change us from our old carnal way of living, thinking, and behaving. These ways are contrary to the philosophies of this existing era, including our vain worldly logic and old religious experiences that many have held in great esteem and some still value in high regards, supposing that our previous worldly viewpoints and reasoning, along with our religious knowledge from past applications, are supposed to be combined, mixed into, or automatically rolled over into this new way of thinking and living. Hebrews (Ivriym) 10:20

Now, the reason why the text documents YAH's way of living and thinking as "new" is because our ancestors (Israel) failed to continually pass on to future generations YAH's laws, statutes, commandments, and customs. So, learning how to execute our true culture and way of life, in this period of time, becomes a challenge because we have grown accustomed to the immoral ways of living in this present world.

And this is why I mentioned earlier in the above readings that many of us (who have come into this truth) have **NOT** been "Truly Converted." Robotically, we assume just because we are descendants of a great people whom YAH has chosen and deems special that makes us automatically set apart without anything else being required of us from the MOST HIGH, as noted in the writings of Micah (Miykah) 6:2 and 8:

"Hear ye, O mountains, for YAH's controversy, and ye strong foundations of the earth: for YAH hath a controversy with his people, and he will *plead with Israel.*"

"He hath shewed thee, O man (or people as prospectively noted throughout the entire chapter referring to HIS people Israel), what is good; and what doth YAH require of thee, but to do justly (following his path of righteousness and not your own), to love mercy, and to walk humbly with YAH thy power?"

One of the greatest examples of this is from the story of our beloved brother, patriarch, and apostle Simeon, also known as Peter (Kepha) who, after being spiritually awakened (as an Hebrew) by the Messiah in his personal aspirations to follow after the MOST HIGH, there was still a tremendous necessity for him (Peter) to be converted, to no longer walk/live after the ways of his own flesh, conforming to the mindset of his present society, but to walk after the ways of YAH's spirit by being transformed in the renewing of his mind.

Change is a process, but we must be willing to accept it and conform to it. Although Peter was called, he was still overly concerned about his fishing profession (his worldly endeavors) to the point it took precedence over and above his purpose in YAH and the HaMaschiach. And while his actions showed a desire toward the Most High, in the time of trouble and pressure, he would deny the Messiah as we sometimes do by our present actions. And this is what the Messiah stated to Peter:

"But I have prayed for thee, that thy faith fail not: and when thou art <u>"CONVERTED,"</u> strengthen thy brethren." Luke (Lucas) 22:32 (KJV)

"So when they had dined, the Messiah saith to Simon Peter, 'Simon, son of Jonas, lovest thou me more than these things?' He saith unto him, 'Yea Messiah, thou knowest that I love thee.' He saith unto him, 'Feed my lambs.'" John (Yahuchanon) 21:15 (KJV)

"The Messiah answered and said unto him (Judas), 'If a man love me, <u>he will keep my words</u>: and my Father will love him, and we will come unto him, and make our abode with him.'" John (Yahuchanon) 14:23

So, in essence, the results of someone who is truly converted is the act of loving the Most High more than their own personal earthly achievements and desires, and the fruit from this behavior will be one who will strive to keep the Messiah's words, sayings, and commandants (in context) without excuses.

And in the process of time when Simon Peter was fully converted (which doesn't mean he was completely faultless), but it does mean he conformed to YAH's ways by virtue of HIS statutes, laws, and commandments through his Spirit. He strengthened other believing Hebrews with this message:

"Repent ye therefore, and <u>BE CONVERTED</u>, that your sins may be blotted out, when the times of refreshing shall come from the presence of YAH." Acts (Ma'aseh) 3:19 (KJV)

And it's with true repentance by means of spiritual adjustments and physical applications that our sins (which are a transgressions of YAH's laws, both past and present) can truly be blotted out. In return, we'll be refreshed and reenergized day after day by the Spirit of the Most High (through the Ruach HaKodesh).

Furthermore, being converted extends far beyond following only the ritual elements of the law, such as adding tassels to our outer garments. It's much more detailed than that, especially when applying the aspects of the law with only a carnal understanding.

And this is the plight in which Paul wrote so many letters in continual disputes with the leaders of our people pertaining to application of the laws. Paul taught that the law is spiritual and good, but also harmful when used subsequent to the flesh and not in harmony with the Spirit of YAH.

In addition, this is why the Messiah noted in the book of Matthew (Mattithyahu) 5:20 (NLT):

**"But I warn you – unless your righteousness is better than the righteousness of the teachers of religious law and the Pharisees,**

you will never enter the Kingdom of Heaven."

This statement was not made for us to imitate their deeds but rather as a warning to avoid such behavior, as noted by the Messiah:

"They crush people with unbearable religious demands and never lift a finger to ease the burden." Matthew (Mattithyahu) 23:v.4 (NLT)

"Every thing that they do is for show (the outward show of the flesh to be seen of men). On their arms they wear extra-wide prayer boxes with Scripture verses inside, and they wear robes with extra-long tassels..." v.5 (KJV)

"They love to receive respectful greetings as they walk in the marketplaces and to be called "Rabbi"...v.6 (KJV)

Woe (what sorrow awaits) you scribes and Pharisees, hypocrites! For ye are like unto white sepulchers (or washed tombstones), which indeed appear beautiful outwardly, but are within full of dead men's bones, and all uncleanness"...v.27 (KJV)

**Even so ye also outwardly appear "RIGHTEOUS" unto men, but within ye are full of hypocrisy and iniquity...v.28 (KJV)**

This was the true meaning behind the statement that was made by the Messiah regarding the religious teachers of the law when he stated **"except your righteousness exceed the righteousness of the scribes and Pharisees, ye shall in no case enter into the kingdom of heaven.** Matthew (Mattithyahu) 5:20 (KJV)

Because their righteousness was solely a reflection in their outer garments with embroidered Scriptures and long beautiful tassels (and I will add, head coverings) – the exterior works of the flesh – i.e., standing in the marketplaces to be seen of men for reputation, etc., while the inner man – the spiritual moral law of the people were being abandoned and forsaken – leaving one spiritually dead in their sins, blind, unclean, and devoid of spiritual truth.

The righteousness of YAH is not merely what we have on us, but what we have in us – which will ultimately reflect on/in our lives.

# 1
# THE MOSAIC & ETERNAL LAW

In light of understanding the Mosaic Law, although it appears to be very simple to comprehend, it is actually more complex than one may imagine or think. This is because while many of the laws involve physical applications, the LAW itself requires spiritual discernment in order to properly execute.

**"For we know that the law is spiritual: but I am (or we are) carnal, sold under sin.** Romans (Romaiym) 7:14 (KJV)

**"So the trouble is not with the law, for it is spiritual and good. The trouble is with me (or us), for I am (or we are) all too human, a slave to sin.** Romans (Romaiym) 7:14 (NLT)

Many of our people do not possess the Ruach HaKodesh for guidance (the set-apart Spirit) for various reasons and beliefs; therefore, the law is often applied (solely) with a fleshly and carnal perception. And this will be fully discussed in the next chapter.

For example, based on the above scriptural text, many of our people associate the wearing of tassels as spiritual or that the tassels themselves ARE the Spirit. However, the wearing of tassels is merely a reminder to observe and obey the:

- Moral Laws
- Civil Laws
- Ceremonial Laws
- Dietary Laws
- Social Laws

**"The tassels will help you (or assist you) in remembering that you must obey all my commands and be set apart to YAH.** Numbers (Bemidbar) 15:40 (NLT)

But today, the tassel is viewed as part of Israel's redemption and eternal salvation, and more weight, honor and respect is given to the wearing of tassels on our outer garments rather than to the obedience of faith.

So, let's get into some of the Paul's writings because for many of our people, it is through his writings that a lot of us become confused as we were warned by Simon (Peter) when he noted:

"This is what our beloved brother Paul also wrote to you with the wisdom YAH gave him – speaking of these things in all of his letters.

Some of his comments are hard to understand, and those who are ignorant and unstable have twisted his letters to mean something quite different, just as they do with other parts of Scripture. And this will result in their destruction." 2 Peter (Kepha) 3:16 (NLT)

Paul **NEVER** wrote, taught, or educated anyone about YAH's laws being done away with, or altogether voided, or cancelled out. Although that is the general consensus for many (Christians or people of other faiths/beliefs) which is primarily due to the lack of understanding the covenants that YAH has promised his people. It is also due to the lack of understanding historical background related to the audiences that were being taught by Paul.

Another interesting point is that when people correctly affirm "that Paul was not stating in his writings that the laws are done away with" those who make those arguments usually allow Paul's writing to go unexplained. They'll defend what it's not saying -- while not acknowledging the meanings of his speech.

The apostle's primary fight among his own people was this:

**"Dear brothers and sisters: the longing of my heart and my prayer to YAH for the people of ISRAEL to be saved (restored).**

**I know what enthusiasm they (ISRAEL) have for YAH, but it is misdirected zeal.**

**For they (ISRAEL) don't understand YAH's way of making people right with himself.**

**Refusing to accept YAH's way, they (ISRAEL) cling to their own way of getting right with YAH by trying to keep the law."** Romans (Romaiym) 10:1-3 (NLT)

Paul is not stressing that "trying to keep the law" is wrong, but it is the attempt for many of Israel's so-called elders and teachers in equating the wearing of tassels (just one of the many examples) as the justification of YAH's righteousness.

Paul concluded with…

**"…going about to establish their OWN RIGHTEOUSNESS, they (ISRAEL) have NOT submitted themselves unto the righteousness of YAH."**

Why? Because we (ISRAEL) were called by YAH NOT based on any works of our own that we have done. We were deemed peculiar and noted as being a special people above all Nations – NOT based on our own gifts and talents. But simply because YAH chose us and called us to be so – He justified us (and our ancestors) before the foundations of the world, prior – to the giving of the laws: both spoken and written.

Ephesians (Eph'siym) 1:4: **"Even before he made the world, YAH loved us and chose us in the Messiah to be holy (set apart) and without fault in his eyes."**

So, when the passage states that a man/woman is not justified by the works of the law, but by the faith, and that by the works of the law shall no flesh be justified, Galatians (Galatiym) 2:16; 3:11, it is simply stating that we (ISRAEL) are justified (G1344) which means "to be rendered or declared righteous/set apart" just because YAH pronounced it to be so.

G1344 - *dikaioō*
**Outline of Biblical Usage:**
   I. to render righteous or such he ought to be
   II. to show, exhibit, evince, one to be righteous, such as he is and wishes himself to be considered
   III. to declare, pronounce, one to be just, righteous, or such as he ought to be

So, does that mean we can live and behave in any type of way, and ignore YAH's Laws, and replace it with grace?

**"Do we then make void the law through faith? YAH forbid: yea, we establish or uphold the law."** Romans (Romaiym) 3:31 (KJV)

Again,

**Well then, if we emphasize faith, does this mean that we can forget about the law? Of course not! In fact, only when we have faith do we truly fulfill the law** Romans (Romaiym) 3:31 (NLT).

No, being justified by faith does not give anyone the right to make excuses to live in sin (or in the transgression of the law). In addition, we also are taught to walk (live) by faith and not by sight, knowing that whatsoever is not of faith is (also) sin; as well as that ALL disobedience is a form of sin or transgression of the law. 1 Timothy (Timotheus) 1:9).

Consequently, faith comes from hearing the message, and (in these final days) the message is heard through the WORD of YAH through our Messiah. 1 Corinthians (Qorintiym) 5:7; Romans (Romaiym) 14:23; Romans (Romaiym) 10:17

And although we are declared righteous in the eyes of YAH by faith doesn't eliminate the execution of our obedience to YAH's laws, but rather it (our faith) is upheld/established by not abusing or transgressing the law.

The word "establish" from G2476, means to cause or make to STAND FIRM. To be kept intact, in place, and fixed in the presence of others.

> **G2476 - histēmi**
>
> **Outline of Biblical Usage:**
> I. to cause or make to stand, to place, put, set
>   A. to bid to stand by, [set up]
>     i. in the presence of others, in the midst, before judges, before members of the Sanhedrin;
>     ii. to place
>   B. to make firm, fix establish
>     i. to cause a person or a thing to keep his or its place
>     ii. to stand, be kept intact (of family, a kingdom), to escape in safety
>     iii. to establish a thing, cause it to stand
>       a. to uphold or sustain the authority or force of anything

So, just because we are saved (restored) by grace through faith, not of works lest any man should boast (Ephesians (Eph'siym) 2:8); our faith is maintained and kept intact by the establishment of the laws to the obedience of faith to keep us from living lawlessly and disobediently, becoming sinners and ungodly. (1 Timothy (Timotheus) 1:9).

The word "grace" from G5485, means "that which affords joy, pleasure, and delight from what is due and should be viewed as nothing more than what is known as "a grace period, or better yet, a dispensation that brings YAH pleasure."

### G5485 - *charis*
**Outline of Biblical Usage:**

I. grace
  A. that which affords joy, pleasure, delight, sweetness, charm, loveliness: grace of speech
II. good will, loving-kindness, favour
  A. of the merciful kindness by which God, exerting his holy influence upon souls, turns them to Christ, keeps, strengthens, increases them in Christian faith, knowledge, affection, and kindles them to the exercise of the Christian virtues
III. what is due to grace
  A. the spiritual condition of one governed by the power of divine grace
  B. the token or proof of grace, benefit
    i. a gift of grace
    ii. benefit, bounty
IV. thanks, (for benefits, services,

In other words, the law condemned unrighteous acts and, in many cases, we were destined to die following the unrighteous deeds.

But grace has come, not so that we can continue in the unrighteous acts, but to grant us extended time to correct the unrighteous behaviors (through the Spirit of the Most High), causing one to live in obedience. Grace was never allotted to us as an excuse to continue in transgression of the law or in walking/living in unbelief.

**"What shall we say then? Shall we continue in sin, that grace may abound? YAH forbid. How shall we, that are dead to sin, live any longer therein?"** Romans (Romaiym) 6:1 (KJV)

**"Well then, should we keep on sinning so that YAH can show us more and more of his wonderful grace? Of course not! Since we have died to sin, how can we continue to live in it?"** Romans (Romaiym) 6:1 (NLT)

So, Paul's biggest disgruntlement with his fellow Israelite brothers and sisters wasn't so much about "whether or not we should keep the law," but rather "how the law should be **viewed and maintained**" – not as a badge of self-righteousness, but as a fixture and guide, keeping us in touch and intact in the ways/culture of YAH in the presence and sight of other heathen Nations who are lawless.

And it is IMPOSSIBLE to properly execute YAH's LAWS apart from his Spirit. For our brother Paul (Shau'l) also told us in the book of 1 Corinthians (Qorintiym) 2:14 that:

**"But the natural man (or carnal mind) receiveth not the things of the Spirit of YAH; for they are foolishness unto him: neither can he know them, because they (those things that are spiritual) are spiritually discerned (or requires spiritual assistance and guidance)."**

So, in essence, it was the Spirit of YAH who called Moses to the set-apart mountain and had given him the written (logos) of the laws and explained to him how each and every law was to be implemented. Although Moses was permitted to establish aspects of the law because of the hardness of our hearts (in the example of divorce, etc.), Moses was not permitted to insert or deviate from any regulation or decree that required our full obedience established by YAH.

"So be careful to obey all the commands I give you. You must not add anything to them or subtract anything from them." Deuteronomy (Devariym) 12: 32 (NLT)

And this is why Paul noted in the book of 2 Corinthians (Qorintiym) 3:1-6:

**"This "letter" is written not with pen and ink, but with the Spirit of the living YAH. It is carved not on tablets of stone (the law), but on human hearts."**

**"Who also hath made us able ministers of the New Testament (covenant); not of the letter (of stone), but of the spirit: for the letter killeth, but the spirit gives (it) life."**

Again, our brother wrote things that are hard to understand, and they that are unlearned and unstable twist his letters/writings unto their own destruction. And because we know as Paul mentioned earlier that our faith does not make void the law, the above passage is not an attempt to do away with it (meaning to remove its guidelines).

But Paul was demonstrating that the Mosaic Law interpreted by man – apart from the Spirit of the Most High YAH – does more harm than good to the point that it even kills people's faith; but concluded that the Spirit (of YAH) is what gives life and understanding to properly apply the law. The Spirit of YAH is what gives the law its meaning and definition and consecration and not by the understanding from the natural man's perspective; this is how people are held captive in bondage and turning a culture and lifestyle of a nation into a new religion or sect.

And again, why did YAH stress the importance of not adding to or subtracting from what HE established? Because our natural minds (apart from the Spirit of the Most High Yah himself) cannot comprehend HIS thoughts nor his ways.

HIS established WORD has never returned empty without accomplishing its ordained tasks; neither has it ever failed to complete the mission it was designed to and appointed for. It (His WORD) always had a higher purpose then what has been fully revealed to us. (Isaiah (Yesha'yahu) 55:8-11)

So now, what is the law? This is another thing that's often misconstrued. Maybe I should have started with this at the beginning of this chapter; however, I just went with the flow that was on my mind.

Oftentimes, when you hear the term "laws or commandments," whether or not it's heard from the older or newer writings of our books (Old and New Testament, as often referred to as), it is frequently noted as being solely related to the "Mosaic Laws," which is incomplete in and of itself. Also, there are times when you hear people make statements relative to an act or behavior prior to the writings of Mosaic Law – such as "that was before the law" as a way of noting that YAH's laws did not exist prior to the Mosaic version of the law. This too is also false.

The first five books of our set-apart writings are known as and considered to be "the Torah." And if that's the case – and it is – we have to take note that the books of Genesis (Bereshith) and Jubilees are law-based books prior to the Mosaic Laws. This is what was said about Abraham prior to the coming of the Mosaic Laws:

**"Because that <u>Abraham</u> obeyed my voice, and kept my charge, <u>my commandments</u>, my statutes, and my laws."** Genesis (Bereshith) 26:5 (KJV)

So, this alone debunks the notion that there were no existing laws prior to the laws of Moses. In addition, let's define the words "commandments" and "laws" in this passage:

- Commandment – mitzvah (H4687), means: human and

> ### H4687 - *mitsvah*
> **Strong's Definitions:** מִצְוָה mitsvâh, mits-vaw'; from H6680; a command, whether human or divine (collectively, the Law):— (which was) commanded(-ment), law, ordinance, precept.

divine law, ordinances, precepts.

- Laws – towrah (H8451), means: law, direction, instruction, custom, manners, legal directives: from the Deuteronomy or Mosaic Law to include the **body of prophetic teachings** and **the instructions in the Messianic age or period of time**.

> ### H8451 - *towrah*
> **Outline of Biblical Usage:**
> I. law, direction, instruction
>   A. instruction, direction (human or divine)
>     i. body of prophetic teaching
>     ii. instruction in Messianic age
>     iii. body of priestly direction or instruction
>     iv. body of legal directives
>   B. law
>     i. law of the burnt offering
>     ii. of special law, codes of law
>   C. custom, manner
>   D. the Deuteronomic or Mosaic Law

So, with that being said, then what is the law?

**"And he humbled thee, and suffered thee to hunger, and fed thee with manna, which thou knewest not, neither did thy fathers know; that he might make thee know that man doth not live by bread only, but by <u>EVERY word that proceedeth out of the mouth of YAH</u> doth man live."** Deuteronomy (Devariym) 8:1-3

And during the Messianic period, he echoed those same words found in the books of Matthew (Mattithyahu) 4:4 and Luke (Lucas) 4:4:

**"But he answered and said, It is written, Man shall not live by bread alone, <u>but by every word that proceedeth out of the mouth of YAH</u>."**

And this is where the confusion comes in at times. Due to whenever the words "commandments" and "laws" are shown in Scripture text, whether in what we know as the "Old or New Testament," it is only linked or fused with the Mosaic Laws.

Any words that flowed from the mouth of the Most High YAH via his angels, prophets, or the Messiah, were directives, ordinances, instructions, etc. Anything that proceeded from the mouth of the Most High were not opinions or options that were debatable.

There are many examples in our writings of our people being punished/destroyed for taking the Most High's words lightly, such as the example of our brother Achan, from the tribe of Judah, who disobeyed the message of YAH that proceeded from his messenger Joshua. Joshua (Yashusha) 6 and 7:

**"Joshua commanded the people, 'Shout! For the Most High has given you the town! Jericho and everything in it must be completely destroyed as an offering to the Most High.**

Only Rahab the prostitute (Harlot) and the others in her house will be spared, for she protected our spies.

**Do not take any of the things set apart for destruction, or you yourselves will be completely destroyed, and you will bring trouble on the camp of Israel.'"** Joshua (Yashusha) 6:16; 18 (NLT)

**"But the children of Israel committed a trespass in the accursed**

thing: for Achan, the son of Carmi, the son of Zabdi, the son of Zerah, of the tribe of Judah, took of the accursed thing: and the anger of the MOST HIGH kindled against the children of Israel." Joshua (Yashusha) 7:1 (KJV)

And although this was not written in what we would call "the Torah," nor that it was written as one of the 613 commandments in the Mosaic Law, doesn't mean that the YAH's set-apart instructions were open for personal interpretation on whether or not it should be obeyed. And my main point is that we, the nation of Israel, should be striving to live by "**Every word** that comes forth out of the mouth of YAH and not just some parts of it," which as we see, not striving to follow all of YAH's instructions will cause us to violate some.

Let's look further in this understanding! It is noted in the book of Luke (Lucas) 6:47:

**"As for everyone who comes to me and hears my words (sayings) and puts them into practice, I will show you what they are like..."**

The meaning of "words" or "sayings" found in this passage comes from G3056) logos which means "a word uttered by a living voice;

embodies a conception or idea. It also means "what is declared, a thought, a weighty saying, etc."

> **G3056 - *logos***
>
> **Outline of Biblical Usage:**
> I. of speech
>   A. a word, uttered by a living voice, embodies a conception or idea
>   B. what someone has said
>     i. a word
>     ii. the sayings of God
>     iii. decree, mandate or order
>     iv. of the moral precepts given by God
>     v. Old Testament prophecy given by the prophets
>     vi. what is declared, a thought, declaration, aphorism, a weighty saying, a dictum, a maxim

So, when the Messiah uttered these words found in the book of John (Yahuchanon) 14:15; 23-24:

**"If ye love me, keep my commandments."**

"The Messiah answered and said unto him, If a man love me, he will <u>keep my words</u>: and my Father will love him, and we will come unto him, and make our abode with him.

He that loveth me not keepeth not <u>my sayings</u>: and the word which ye hear is not mine, but the Father's which sent me."

He was not exclusively referencing "the Mosaic Law" as much as he was referencing His words, His sayings, and His commandments, the words that were uttered from His "Living Voice" in declaring a thought or a weighty saying. It's very rare to hear many quote this statement from the Messiah: "If a man love me, he will **KEEP MY WORDS**" rather than the plethora of people who quote the verse from the book of John (Yahuchanon) 14:15 to solely mean **"the Mosaic Laws"** and disregard the true meaning of that passage, which leans toward the living words that flowed from the mouth of the Messiah to his disciples and people during that period of his life.

So, we have to be very careful not to view every passage of Scripture when the following terms are being used: "commandments, precepts, law, words, sayings, instructions, etc., as solely meaning "The Mosaic Laws" without verifying the meaning with application to the proper context in which the word is being used.

For example:

**"Then what becomes of our boasting? It is excluded. By what kind of law? By a law of works? No, but by the law of faith."** Romans (Romaiym) 3:27

The *Thyer's Greek Lexicon (3551)* describes the word "law" in this text as being anything established, anything received by usage, a custom. It goes on to note in this particular passage it denotes a law or rule producing a state approved by YAH, i.e., by the observance of which we are approved by YAH.

**"In my first book, I told you, Theophilus, about everything the Messiah began to do and teach until the day he was taken up to heaven after giving his chosen apostles further instructions (or commandments) through the Holy Spirit (Ruach)."** Acts (Ma'aseh) 1:1-2 (NLT)

So what were those further instructions and commandments given to the Apostles through the Ruach other than what was already transcribed through Moses?

The law of obedience through faith in Yahawashi. In essence, and only by the power and spirit of the Most High, we should be aiming at adhering to the obedience of faith without altogether eliminating or ignoring the tenets of the Torah (in proper context), the writings of the prophets, the psalms, the proverbs, the apocrypha, etc.; lastly and most importantly – the WORD himself, our HaMaschiach, who was manifested in these last days for us. His words are just as important and critical to our well-being and salvation (restoration) than even that of the Mosaic Laws.

I'm not indicating that the sayings and message of the HaMaschiach and the Mosaic Laws are in contrast to each other. Absolutely not, but what Moses could not do, the Messiah could – which was extending the meanings and teaching of the Mosaic Laws and bringing them where they were intended/foreordained to go.

For example, in these passages the Messiah quotes the Mosaic Law first, but then he doesn't teach us to violate the law, but rather he elevates the law to its perfect meaning and understanding – Matthew (Mattithyahu) 5 beginning at verse 21:

"You have heard that our ancestors were told, 'You must not murder. If you commit murder, you are subject to judgment. Exodus (Shemot) 20:13. **But I say,** (elevated) **if you are even angry with someone** (our fellow brothers and sisters of our own nation)**, you are subject to judgment! If you call someone an idiot, you are in danger of being brought before the court. And if you curse someone, you are in danger of the fires of hell."** (NLT)

But all too often, the words of the Messiah are ignored because we see this violation repeated amongst our nation on a daily basis. And we, as a whole, don't practice the next set of passages:

**"So if you are presenting a sacrifice at the altar in the Temple and you suddenly remember that someone has something against you, leave your sacrifice there at the altar. Go and be reconciled to that person. Then come and offer your sacrifice to YAH."**

And because that's not written verbatim in the Torah or the Mosaic Laws, per say, that is often ignored as well. We forget that we are supposed to live by every word, especially of the living WORD himself – even Moses recognized that in his day.

More examples:

"You have heard the commandment that says, 'You must not commit adultery.' Exodus (Shemot) 20:14. But I say, (elevated) anyone who even looks at a woman with lust has already committed adultery with her in his heart."

"You have heard the law that says, 'A man can divorce his wife (for any reason) by merely giving her a written notice of divorce." (Deuteronomy (Devariym) 24:1-5) But I say (elevation) that a man who divorces his wife, unless she has been unfaithful, causes her to commit adultery. And anyone who marries a divorced woman also commits adultery."

And this is why many of our people (fellow Israelites) deny the coming of the Messiah for the sake of continuing to establish Moses, so to speak. But Moses, as well as the tabernacle, was just the pattern, resemblance, and model – the precursor to our Messiah – who was the actual/perfect example and final construction or foundation in which we gain access through a perfect example of living for Abba Father.

There are many places where this is mentioned (Exodus (Shemot)

25:9; 40; 26:30).

"You must build this tabernacle and its furnishings exactly according to the pattern I will show you." (NLT)

Moses, the tabernacle, animal sacrifice, and many other customs were just a pattern or forerunner of the "perfect" which was to come. Note that the word "pattern" means resemblance and model: the precursor.

> ### H8403 - *tabniyth*
>
> **Strong's Definitions:** תַּבְנִית tabnîyth, tab-neeth'; from H1129; structure; by implication, a model, resemblance:— figure, form, likeness, pattern, similitude.

And as I stated earlier, Moses was fully aware of this:

"Then said he unto me, in the bush, I did manifestly reveal myself unto Moses, and talked with him, when my people served in Egypt.

And I sent him and led my people out of Egypt, and brought him up to the mount of where I held him by me a long season.

And told him many wondrous things, and shewed him the secrets of the times, AND THE END; and commanded him saying,

These words shalt thou declare, and these (words) shalt thou hid." 2 Esdras 14:1-6

Moses was fully aware of his purpose as he was shown many wonderful things, and secrets, and the **END TIMES**. This is why (even in his days) Moses proclaimed this statement regarding the coming of the Messiah which was to come and came.

MOSES stated with his own words:

"The MOST HIGH will raise up unto thee a Prophet from the midst of thee, of thy brethren, like unto me; <u>unto him ye SHALL hearken</u>;

I will raise them up a Prophet from among their brethren, like unto thee, and <u>will put my words in his mouth</u>; and he shall speak unto them all that I shall command him.

**And it shall come to pass, that whosoever will not hearken unto my words which he shall speak in my name, I will require it of him."** Deuteronomy (Devariym) 18:15; 18-19

The glory of the Messiah which Moses witnessed on Mount Sinai was the glory that shown on his face when he returned to the people from the mountain. Many Israelites could not gaze upon him because he appeared so different from what they were used to. (Moses' glory was temporary and was abolished for the greater glory which was to come/came through the Messiah and overshadowed that of Moses) – as it is this day. 2 Corinthians (Qorintiym) 3:7-17

Many of our people severely struggle with the torch (so to speak) being passed from Moses to the Messiah, to the point that when anything that pertains to Moses is read; that same veil over his face, is placed over the hearts of some Israelites in denial of the greater glory which comes through the Messiah.

And as the passage continues to state: **"Nevertheless when it (they) turn to the HaMasciach, the veil shall be taken away."** 2Corinthians (Qorintiym) 3:7-17

Again, Moses did not struggle with his purpose of being "a model or precursor" for the Messiah; in fact, this passage is mentioned two more times in context, regarding some who would attempt to use Moses and the "table of stones" as a defense to override and disregard the words of our Messiah that overshadowed the traditions of the Mosaic practices.

This quote comes from the mouth of Simon Peter as he was previously emphasizing prior to this verse the necessity of repentance with conversion and an ear to hear the message of our HaMaschiach:

**"For Moses truly said unto the fathers, A prophet shall the Most High raise up unto you of your brethren, like unto me; <u>"HIM SHALL YE HEAR IN ALL THINGS"</u> whatsoever he shall say unto you."** Acts (Ma'aseh) 3:22 (KJV)

"For Moses truly said unto the fathers, A prophet shall the MOST HIGH raise up unto you of your brethren, like unto me; him shall ye hear in all things whatsoever he shall say unto you.

**And it shall come to pass, that every soul, which will not hear that prophet, shall be destroyed from among the people.**

**Yea, and all the prophets from Samuel and those that follow after, as many as have spoken, have likewise foretold of these days."** Acts (Ma'aseh) 3:22-24 (NLT)

Again.

This message came from Stephen when some of our own zealous people accused him of not following the Law of Moses, for the sake of following the message of the Messiah with guidance from the Ruach:

**"This is that Moses, which said unto the children of Israel, A prophet shall the Lord your God raise up unto you of your brethren, like unto me; him shall ye hear."** Acts (Ma'aseh) 7:37

And ultimately Stephen was stoned because our people refused to hear the voice of the Living Word which flowed through the lips of our Messiah that YAH stated in times past:

**"HE will speak through him and give him words to utter in these last days."** Hebrews (Ivriym) 1:1-2

And presently, out of the numerous commandments you hear stated in the marketplaces, streets, corners, highways, and byways, the very words and commandments that Moses gave to our people **DIRECTLY FROM THE MOST HIGH YAH** in the book of **Deuteronomy 18:15; 18-19** is one of the **most ignored and less mentioned precepts** amongst the gathering of his elect.

So, why are the words, sayings, precepts, and commandments of the Messiah being ignored? Why are his precepts in scriptural passages often used; but never used congruent with his sayings when being essential to our well-being as salvation (restoration)?

And why as a whole do we as a people struggle with the words of the Messiah when his words lead to our eternal state of being with YAH?

In fact, where are the commandments of the Messiah? Well, have you ever read the **book of Matthew chapters 5 through 10**, etc., as well as many other passages where he mentions things like **"when you pray don't be as a hypocrite"**? "When you fast…"? Judge not least you be judged…"?

And I suppose that many ignore his sayings chiefly because those passages of Scripture don't start off with the phrase **"Thou shall not…"** Many conclude (in thought or action) that's how our commandments are supposed to start, in the voice and language of the modern "Old English" dialect.

Although the coming of the Messiah through the era of grace (the extension to living right without the immediate penalty/punishment of death) to the obedience of faith which comes by hearing his sayings (his living precepts declared) and practicing them, is not a license to completely ignore the Mosaic Laws. True repentance first comes by acknowledging our transgression of the laws; and without the established laws (as our schoolmaster) we would have never learned what sin is.

In other words, our people, the nations of Israel, would never be able to reach perfection solely through the works of the Mosaic Law (past and present); but it was those laws that aided us in identifying where we came short of the glory of YAH unto repentance; and now, through the obedience of faith (by hearing, keeping and performing his sayings), we gain access to Abba Father because the Messiah lived what we could not live (the Mosaic Laws) flawlessly without sin.

**"Therefore, since we have a great high priest who has passed through the heavens, YAHAWASHI the Son of YAH, let us hold firmly to what we profess.**

For we do not have a high priest who is unable to sympathize with our weaknesses, but we have one who was tempted in every way that we are, yet was without sin.

**Let us then approach the throne of grace with confidence, so that we may receive mercy and find grace to help us in our time of need."** Hebrews (Ivriym) 4:14-16

Although people will have you to believe that Zechariah and Elizabeth found in the book of Luke (Lucas) 1, never sinned because of this statement:

**"...there was a priest named Zechariah, of the division of Abijah. And he had a wife from the daughters of Aaron, and her name was Elizabeth. And they were both righteous before YAH, walking blamelessly in all the commandments and statutes of the Lord."**

Once again, we know that as a Nation we were justified and declared righteous before the foundation of the world, which also included Zechariah and Elizabeth; but with that justification, they maintained their present state of living without transgression or violation of the law.

However, unlike our Messiah, does this mean that Zechariah and Elizabeth never sinned or never came short of YAH's glory? No, because later on in the text, it states this regarding Zechariah:

**"And behold, you will be silent and unable to speak until the day that these things take place, because <u>you did not believe my words</u>, which will be fulfilled in their time."**

As it is stated under the Laws of Moses, "sin is a transgression of the law," so it is also under the obedience of faith in the Messiah that's noted by his apostles:

**"...whatsoever is not of faith is (also) sin."** Romans (Romaiym):14:23

Although, the subject of discussion was centered around food, we all know that living and walking by faith extends far beyond (chicken and collard greens) food.

And what was shown regarding Zechariah was that although noted he walked blamelessly in the commandments, this same man, fell short in walking by faith (which is also a form of sin) wherein he struggled in believing the words given to him through the messenger of the MOST HIGH.

And as we see in the story where Zechariah was silenced by the angel of YAH because he didn't believe what he was told and his mouth was sealed shut to keep him from sinning with his lips and tongue in the same manner in which the prophet Isaiah sinned. Isaiah (Yesha'yahu) 6:5

This is why the book of Hebrews (Ivriym) 3:1-15 illustrates this point:

"And so, dear brothers and sisters who belong to YAH and are partners with those called to heaven, think carefully about this Messiah whom we declare to be YAH's messenger and High Priest.

For he (the HaMaschiach) was faithful to YAH, who appointed him, just as Moses served faithfully when he was entrusted with YAH's entire house.

But the Messiah deserves far more glory than Moses, just as a person who builds a house deserves more praise than the house itself. For every house has a builder, but the one who built everything is YAH.

Moses was certainly faithful in YAH's house as a servant. His work was an illustration of the truths the Most High would reveal later.

But the HaMaschiach, as the Son, is in charge of YAH's entire house. And we are YAH's house, if we keep our courage and remain confident in our hope in the Anointed One.

That is why the Ruach HaKodesh says, "Today when you hear his voice (the Messiah's), don't harden your hearts."

So, as some will correctly ask, "Did the Messiah live by and was obedient to the Mosaic Law, and if so why?"

"But when the set time had fully come, YAH sent his Son, born of a woman, <u>born under the law</u> (why??) to redeem those under the law, that we might receive adoption to sonship." Galatians (Galatiym) 4:4-5 (NLT)

"YAH presented the Messiah as a sacrifice of atonement through the shedding of his blood (why??) – to be received by faith. He did this to demonstrate his righteousness, because in his forbearance he had left the sins committed beforehand unpunished (the penalties of our sins from breaking the law).

**He did it to demonstrate his righteousness at the present time, so as to be just and the one who justifies those who have faith in the Messiah."** Romans (Romaiym) 3:25-26


Again, this is why the Messiah cannot be received by some Israelites, because they refuse to allow the glory of the Messiah to overshadow the glory that was given to Moses.


**"The old way, with laws etched in stone, led to death, though it began with such glory."** 2 Corinthians (Qorintiym) 3:7


We know this is not saying that the law is death, because we recognize that it's spiritual; and we also understand that the wages of sin leads to death. Romans (Romaiym) 6:23


So, when the law was given to us as a people, it revealed our deep dark sins. Instead of us coming clean, many of us clung to sin (because we became slaves to our transgressions – as it is this day), which eventually worked in us all manner of ways that led to death (physically, spiritually, emotionally, and socially).

Some of us were so far gone in our customs that we even found ways to use the law (partially) in transgression to its original purpose. Such as in the case found in the book of Malachi (Mal'akiy) 1:7-8, where the priests offered sacrifices to the Most High YAH, albeit, they offered the worst of the animals (the sick, blind, and lame). This was not what YAH required, although they could say **"We did offer a sacrifice."**

And to many of our people that is enough, just having a form of godliness, a look of spirituality without the power of the Most High. 2 Timothy (Timotheus) 3:5

And in the case of Isaiah (Yesha'yahu) 1:3-4, the Most High noted Israel as **"sinful nations,"** a people laden with iniquity, a seed of evildoers, with children that are corrupters."

But that still didn't stop Israel from practicing and participating in worship, feast days celebrations, Sabbaths, New Moons, etc. Isaiah (Yesha'yahu) 1:12-14

Paul also noted Israel's "sinful nation" status in the book of 1Corinthians (Qorintiym) 10:5-7:

**"Yet YAH was not pleased with most of them, and their bodies were scattered in the wilderness. These things happened as a warning to us, so that we would not crave evil things as they did, or worship idols as some of them did. As the Scriptures say, "The people celebrated with feasting and drinking, and they indulged in pagan revelry." (NLT)**

But we as a people love customs. We love to look the part and dress well – but the MOST HIGH requires more just fleshly customs that allow us to play and look the part.

And although Moses' era was glorious with all of its customs, how much more should we look to honor the glory of our Messiah?

**"Shouldn't we expect far greater glory under the new way, now that the YAH is giving life? (Or discernment in the spirit through the aid of the Ruach)**

If the old way, which brings condemnation, was glorious, how much more glorious is the new way, which makes us right with

YAH! In fact, that first glory was not glorious at all compared with the overwhelming glory of the new way.

**So if the old way, which has been replaced, was glorious, how much more glorious is the new, which remains forever!" I Corinthians (Qorintiym) 3:8-11**

And here's where another problem exists:

**"Since this new way gives us such confidence, we can be very bold. We are not like Moses, who put a veil over his face so the people of Israel would not see the glory, even though it was destined to fade away.**

But the people's minds were hardened, and to this day whenever the old covenant is being read, the same veil covers their minds so they cannot understand the truth.

**And this veil can be removed only by believing in our Anointed One (our HaMaschiach).**

Yes, even today when they read Moses' writings, their hearts are covered with that veil, and they do not understand (the ways of the Messiah through the Spirit)."

In addition, this is why the Apostle Paul made these types of statements:

**"Therefore let it be known to you, brothers, that through the Messiah – the forgiveness of sins is proclaimed to you. Through Him everyone who believes is justified (or forgiven) from everything you could not be justified (or forgiven for) from by the Law of Moses."** Acts (Ma'aseh) 13:38-39

"Now we know that whatever the Law [of Moses] says, it speaks to those who are under the Law (the Nation of Israel), so that [the excuses of] every mouth may be silenced [from protesting] and that all the world may be held accountable to YAH [and subject to His judgment].

**For no person will be justified [freed of guilt and declared righteous] in His sight by [solely trying to do] the works of the Law.**

**For through the Law we become conscious of sin [and the recognition of sin directs us toward repentance, but provides no remedy for sin]."** Romans (Romaiym) 3:19-20

Why did the writer note that the Law provided no true remedy for sin? Because of this:

**"For it is not possible that the blood of bulls and of goats should take away sin."** Hebrews (Ivriym) 10:4

Continuing with connected scriptural passages:

"But now the righteousness of YAH has been clearly revealed [independently and completely] apart from the Law, though it is [actually] confirmed by the Law and the [words and writings of the] Prophets.

**"This righteousness of YAH comes through faith in the Messiah for all those who [believe and trust in Him and acknowledge Him as YAH's Son]. There is no distinction, since all have sinned and continually fall short of the glory of YAH. (amongst all Israelites; the Jews and Hellenized Hebrews (Gentiles); those from the Southern and Northern Kingdoms)"** Romans (Romaiym) 3:21-23

**"Do we, then, nullify the law by this faith? Certainly not! Instead, we uphold the law."** Romans (Romaiym) 3:31

How do we uphold the law by faith? By walking in the words of the Spirit of YAH (producing fruit) and not living according to the sinful nature of the flesh is how we uphold, establish, and fulfill the requirement of the law as the Messiah also fulfilled the law.

**"…in order that the righteous requirement of the law might be fully met in us, who do not live according to the flesh but according to the Spirit."** Romans (Romaiym) 8:4

"Meaning that being justified (made right in YAH's sight) by faith does not cancel out the penalties of transgressing the law, for the law was not made or intended to justify or reward righteous acts, but to punish the lawbreaker and evildoer, and the disobedient." (1 Timothy (Timotheus) 1:9)

For the Law is Spiritual because the Word and Essence of YAH is heavenly and invisible to the naked eye until it is manifested for all to see. YAH's eternal and perpetual law is EVERY word that comes from HIS mouth, whether divinely spoken or written, in earlier times and at the present moment.

# 2

# THE RUACH HAKODESH

MY wife and I once asked someone, "What is the overall purpose of the Ruach HaKodesh,"? The response was, "For the purposes of working miracles." At this point, I realized that many of our people who have been awakened to our true heritage may not know the overall purposes and promises of the set-apart Spirit (the Ruach HaKodesh, taught to many as the Holy Spirit/Ghost).

And before we dive deep into the topic, let us not even worry about the foolish jesting from the teachings of Catholicism and Christianity when attempting to incorporate the ideology of whether or not the Ruach HaKodesh is the third person of the man-made trinity doctrine. It's a foolish argument because the Spirit of the Most High has always been. Even our brother Esdras in his days longed to be filled with the set-apart Spirit:

"But if I have found grace before thee, send the Holy Ghost into me, and I shall write all that hath been done in the world since the beginning, which were written in thy law, that men may find thy path, and that they which will live in the latter days may live." 2 Esdras 14:22

One of the most important goals of this discussion is attempting to answer the following questions that our people ponder:

- Who is the set-apart Spirit?
- What is the overall purpose of the set-apart Spirit?
- Who is the set-apart Spirit given to?
- Do we even need the set-apart Spirit?

Over the past several years, one interesting fact that I've gained is that a lot of our people do not even see the need of the Ruach HaKodesh. The last time our people as a Nation rejected the set-apart Spirit, we found ourselves wandering in ignorance in the wilderness for 40 years.

In the last days and moments of our HaMaschiach (the Messiah) in the flesh, he gathered his disciples together and expressed this to them:

"But the Advocate, the Holy Spirit (Ruach HaKodesh), whom the Father will send in My name, will teach you all things and will remind you of everything I have told you." John (Yahuchanon) 14:26

I would like to drop a few nuggets for those who can receive them. If part of the Ruach's overall responsibility is to **remind us** of **"all things"** then tell me what is the purpose of wearing the tassels in this period of time? For the purpose of the tassels was to **remind us of all the things** that were commanded in the Law of Moses.

And furthermore, part of the Ruach's responsibility was to not only remind us of all things, but to also **teach us all things** that the Messiah has instructed those who hear his voice.

As earlier noted in the previous chapter, I see many so-called Hebrew teachers state that when the Messiah spoke these words found in the book of John (Yahuchanon) 14:15. "**If you love me, keep my commandments.**" People will view that as meaning obedience to the Mosaic Law only, which is not fully correct.

When the Messiah spoke those words, he was referring to this, which is found in the same chapter:

"If anyone loves me, he will keep my word, and my Father will love him, and we will come to him and make our home with him. Whoever does not love me does not keep my words. And the word that you hear is not mine but the Father's who sent me." John (Yahuchanon) 14:23-24


Again, this was revealed to Moses beforehand, and Moses himself gave this commandment that:


"'The Most High will raise up for you a Prophet like me from among your OWN people. Listen carefully to EVERYTHING he tells you.'" Deuteronomy (Devariym) 18:15; 18-19


So, in the book of John (Yahuchanon) 14:23-24, the terms "words" or "sayings" in this passage come from: (G3056) logos, which means "a word uttered by a living voice; embodies a conception or idea." It also means "what is declared, a thought, a weighty saying, etc."


So, the Messiah is not teaching us or telling us to disobey the Laws of Moses, but rather to hear in voice and observe his sayings in these last days, and because the Messiah never disobeyed any of the Laws of Moses, he will never teach us the same.

And this will be difficult to understand and receive for many if a person does not possess the Ruach HaKodesh within them as their guide and helper, as noted by the Messiah himself:

**"And I will ask the Father, and he will give you another Helper, to be with you forever, even the Spirit of truth, whom the world cannot receive, because it neither sees him nor knows him. You know him, for he dwells with you and will be in you."** John (Yahuchanon) 14:16-17

And the word "world" (kosmos) in this passage is not exclusive to the heathens, but to the "unbelieving class of people" pertaining to the arranged governmental order of the Nation of Israel, similar to how the word "world" is used in the passage of John 3:16 – pertaining to the Nation of Israel.

And as we continue, the Scriptures themselves will show that the people of his own nation, Hebrew Israelites, are those who rejected him (in obedience to HIS sayings) and his set-apart Spirit (Ruach HaKodesh) in obedience to His purpose).

In the same manner, when you read the book of Genesis (Bereshith) 1:1, it states how the Father created the heavens and the earth; then verse 2 and on demonstrates the actual events of what was spoken in verse 1. It's the same way Acts 1:1-3 should be viewed; then verses 4 and so on tells the story, or is revealing verses 1-3.

"In the first book, O Theophilus, I have dealt with all that the Messiah began to do and teach until the day when he was taken up, after he had given commands through the Holy Spirit to the apostles whom he had chosen.

He presented himself alive to them after his suffering by many proofs, appearing to them during forty days and speaking about the kingdom of YAH.

"And while staying with them he ordered (or commanded) them not to depart from Jerusalem, but to wait for the promise of the Father, which, he said, "you heard from me; for John baptized with water, but you will be baptized with the Holy Spirit not many days from now." Acts (Ma'aseh) 1:4-5

The baptism of the Ruach HaKodesh is not an option of choice, but was commanded by the Messiah in the last days of his physical existence while he was here on earth. And as we have read earlier, he admonished, ordered, and commanded his disciples to tarry and wait during the day of Pentecost (the feast of Harvest) for the baptism of this Spirit.

Again, for what purpose?

**"But the Advocate, the Holy Spirit, whom the Father will send in My name, will teach you all things and will remind you of everything I have told you."** John (Yahuchanon) 14:26

And this is one of the many reasons that "Awakened Israel" is in so much disorder and confusion pertaining to what we are supposed to be doing in these last days, prior to the return of Israel's priesthood and kingdomship (led by our Messiah) as the head and not the tail in the earth, so to speak. Knowing that only a remnant of the entire nation of Israel will be saved (or restored or salvaged): which is the **mystery** behind the passage of Scripture that states, **"all Israel will be saved."** And that we will cover later on in the book.

So, now that we covered both the necessity and the purpose of the set-apart Spirit, who is the set-apart Spirit? And how do we obtain him? And in all simplicity the answer is straightforward.

**"We are witnesses of these things and so is the Holy Spirit (Ruach HaKodesh), who is given by YAH to all those who obey him."** Acts (Ma'aseh) 5:32

The Ruach HaKodesh is given to all of YAH's chosen people (his election, the remnant who will believe). Founded on the obedience of faith based on those who will hear the voice (words) of our Messiah and do them, while not excluding but upholding the tenets of the morality laws, etc., which is the platform by which our faith is broadened or extended.

**"Let me ask you this one question: Did you receive the Holy Spirit (Ruach) by obeying the law of Moses? Of course not! You received the Spirit because you believed the message you heard about the Messiah. How foolish can you be? After starting your new lives in the Spirit, why are you now trying to become perfect by your own human efforts!** (solely based on the works of the law) Galatians (Galatiym) 3:2-3 (NLT)

In other words, the Ruach HaKodesh is given to all those who obey YAH (who opens the conscience of our spiritual understanding), which is tied to compliance to the Words of the Messiah. Then our obedience is displayed through the message, words, and laws of YAH in upholding our faith.

And although the book of Acts notes that the Ruach HaKodesh will be given by YAH to those who obey him, let's closely examine the nature of that Spirit.

**"But you are not controlled by your sinful nature. You are controlled by the Spirit if you have the <u>Spirit of YAH living in you</u>. (And remember that those who do not have the Spirit of Christ [the comforter – the helper – the Ruach]) living in them do not belong to him at all.)**

And if the <u>Messiah lives within you</u>, so even though your body will die because of sin, the Spirit gives you life because you have been made right with YAH.

**The Spirit of YAH, who raised the Messiah from the dead, lives in you. And just as YAH raised the Anointed One from the dead, he will give life to your mortal bodies by this same Spirit living within you."** Romans (Romaiym) 8:9-11

And for those who would try to confuse you by asking, "Well, is the

Spirit of the Father in us, or the Spirit of the Messiah?" The answer is quite simple and the same answer that he stated to his disciples when they were confused by similar statements is the same answer to those who would try to use this statement as a contradiction.

**"Don't you believe that I am in the Father and the Father is in me? The words I speak are not my own, but my Father who lives in me does his work through me."** John (Yahuchanon) 14:10

The same spirit that dwelt in the Messiah (from the Father) is the same spirit (a portion) that lives in us, who teaches, guides us, and directs us in the way of truth in these last days, as it pertains to the Kingdom of YAH and the glory that will be revealed through us and in us.

**"For the Kingdom of YAH is not a matter of what we eat or drink, but of living a life of goodness and peace and joy in the Holy Spirit (Ruach). If you serve the Messiah with this attitude, you will please YAH, and others will approve of you, too."** Romans (Romaiym) 14:17-18

And when you read the earlier passages leading up to this verse, the whole emphasis was based on "certain days to honor" – regarding ceremonial days and "certain foods to eat" – on the topic of the feast day celebrations – pertaining to what to eat and when."

The message was being brought to the attention of new believers of Hebrew origin, in many cases, Greek-speaking Hebrews, who were unfamiliar with and unaccustomed to all the rules and regulations pertaining to the Mosaic Law.

**"In those days when the number of disciples was increasing, the Hellenistic Jews among them complained against the Hebraic Jews because their widows were being overlooked in the daily distribution of food."** Acts (Ma'aseh) 6:1 (NLT)

In most of the writings I'm able to transcribe by Abba Father, I often make the attempt over and over to explain to those who have never heard it before the history of "Hellenism" and how it has severely impacted our people.

Hellenistic (Greek or Grecian): Ἑλληνιστής, ἑλληνιστου, ὁ (from ἑλληνίζω means to copy the manners and worship of the Greeks or to use the Greek language (*Winers Grammar*, 94 (89f), cf. 28), a Hellenist, i.e., one who imitates the manners and customs or the worship of the Greeks, and uses the Greek tongue; **employed in the New Testament of Jews born in foreign lands and speaking Greek (Grecian Jews) and also referred to as "Gentiles."**

> ### G1675 - *Hellēnistēs*
>
> **Outline of Biblical Usage:**
> I. a Hellenist
>   A. one who imitates the manners and customs or the worship of the Greeks, and use the Greek tongue
>   B. used in the NT of Jews born in foreign lands and speaking Greek
>
> **KJV Translation Count:** 3x
> **The KJV translates Strongs G1675 in the following manner:** Grecians (3x).
>
> **Strong's Definitions:** Ἑλληνιστής Hellēnistés, hel-lay-nis-tace'; from a derivative of G1672; a Hellenist or Greek-speaking Jew:—Grecian.

Simon Peter's primary appointment, or what we would call "ministry," pertained to the "Jews," (the circumcised) primarily but not subjected only to the Southern Kingdom (Judah, Benjamin, and a portion of Levi).

Paul's primary appointment, or what we would call "ministry," pertained to the "Gentiles" (not so much relating to the "non-Hebraic" Gentiles) but the scattered Northern Kingdom tribes of

Israel – those Hebrew ancestors who forsook the covenants and customs of their fathers to copy the manners and worship of the Greeks – (the uncircumcised of our people) who were scattered amongst the Gentile nations and considered Gentiles.

**"In those days went there out of Israel wicked men, who persuaded many, saying, Let us go and make a covenant with the heathen that are round about us: for since we departed from them we have had much sorrow. So this device pleased them well.**

Then certain of the people were so forward herein, that they went to the king, who gave them license to do after the ordinances of the heathen: Whereupon they built a place of exercise at Jerusalem according to the customs of the heathen:

**And made themselves <u>uncircumcised</u>, and forsook the holy covenant, and joined themselves to the heathen, and were sold to do mischief."** 1 Maccabees 1:11-15

"Neither was it lawful for a man to keep Sabbath days or ancient fasts, or to profess himself at all to be a Jew." 2 Maccabees 6:6

"Confess him before the Gentiles, ye children of Israel: for he hath scattered us among them. There declare his greatness, and extol him before all the living: for YAH is our Ruler, and he is the Mighty One of our fathers for ever.

And he will scourge us for our iniquities, and will have mercy again, and *will gather us out of all nations*, among whom *he hath scattered us.*" Tobit 13:3-5


Observe closely with me what the Most High was truly ordaining the apostle Paul to do, as noted in the book of Acts (Ma'aseh) 9:15:


"Go, for Saul is my chosen instrument to take my message to the Gentiles (the Hellenized Hebrews scattered among the nations, who were not called Jews) and to kings (those in authority over our people in releasing our people, as in the days of Moses, to freely worship our Heavenly Father in spirit and in truth), as well as to the people of Israel (the stubborn Israelites who, although they obtained their language and culture, rejected the Messiah and Ruach)."

Albeit interesting enough, the Apostle Paul could not begin his ordained assignment until this had occurred:

"So Ananias went and found Saul. He laid his hands on him and said, "Brother Saul, the Messiah, who appeared to you on the road, has sent me so that you might regain your sight and be filled with the Holy Spirit (Ruach).

Instantly something like scales fell from Saul's eyes, and he regained his sight. Then he got up and was baptized." Acts (Ma'aseh) 9:16-17

Another interesting thing about Paul is that he was a Hebrew Israelite from the tribe of Benjamin, well-versed in the Law of Moses, and he upheld it tightly according to the traditions learned from his forefathers. Yet he did not know the Messiah nor could he be recognized by his voice prior to his conversion, as noted by his own account and testimony:

"Then Paul said, "I am a Jew, born in Tarsus, a city in Cilicia, and I was brought up and educated here in Jerusalem under Gamaliel.

As his student, I was carefully trained in the strictness of our Jewish laws and customs. I became very zealous to honor YAH in everything I did, just like all of you today. And I persecuted the followers of the Way, hounding some to death, arresting both men and women and throwing them in prison.

**The high priest and the whole council of elders can testify that this is so. For I received letters from them to our Jewish brothers in Damascus, authorizing me to bring the followers of the Way from there to Jerusalem, in chains, to be punished."** Acts (Ma'aseh) 22:3-5

"The Followers of the Way" (or as noted in other versions of biblical literature, "the People of the Way") was a term that many zealous Hebrews called those disciples who followed the strict teachings of the Messiah (who was also known as "*The Way*, Truth, and Life). (John (Yahuchanon) 14:6)

By Paul's own admission, he persecuted other believing Hebrews who accepted as truth the teachings of the Messiah through the obedience of faith and the Ruach HaKodesh, which the tenets of Law of Moses did not state as a requirement or necessity (the indwelling receiving of the Spirit). Again, although Paul was well-versed in the customs of our law, he did not know the Spirit that governs the law.

"As I was on the road, approaching Damascus about noon, a very bright light from heaven suddenly shone down around me. I fell to the ground and heard a voice saying to me, 'Saul, Saul, why are you persecuting me?'

Then I asked, '<u>**WHO ARE YOU**</u>?'" Acts (Ma'aseh) 22:6-8

And this type of behavior was not new for many of our people, including some of our Hebrew priests who taught the Torah but were void of spiritual understanding and did not know the Spirit that presided over the law.

"But when you (Israel) came in, you defiled my land and made my heritage an abomination. The priests did not say or inquire about: 'Where is the Spirit of the Most High?'

And those priests who handle the law (Torah) – did not know me; the shepherds transgressed against me; the prophets prophesied

**by Baal and went after things that do not profit."** Jeremiah (Yirmeyahu) 2:7-8

And this behavior by far was, mostly, the biggest opposition and brawl throughout the entire book of Acts, which described the "Actions of the Apostles." Those Hebrew Israelites who possessed the Ruach HaKodesh and upheld the obedience of faith without violating the most important commandments – in which all the other commandments are based upon. Matthew (Mattithyahu) 22:40)

Other Hebrews followed hard after the Laws of Moses (as a justification of self-righteousness) while rejecting the teachings of the Messiah (by the way of unbelief or disobedience) and the Ruach HaKodesh.

Not understanding that the Messiah was to be honored in greater glory and respect than Moses and all of the earlier prophets, priests, and kings.

For a new priesthood, extending from the line of "Judah" through the Messiah, was rewriting and promoting a better covenant than the one that was previously established, in which we, as a people, failed to achieve that began through the Levitical priesthood.

**"For when there is a change in the priesthood (from Levi to Judah), there is of necessity a change of the law (concerning the priesthood) as well."** Hebrews (Ivriym) 7:12 (AMP)

**"When YAH speaks of a "new" covenant, it means he has made the first one obsolete. It is now out of date and will soon disappear."** Hebrews (Ivriym) 8:13 (NLT)

And that's why in many cases when the Messiah states to "keep his commandments, his sayings, and his words" (as noted in John 14-15, etc.) by definition and context; is NOT always a reference to the "Laws of Moses" (but not in violation of them either). But rather, it is practicing and performing every word that proceeds out of his mouth.

In addition, this is what the Messiah meant when he told his disciples that "the Ruach HaKodesh, whom the Father will send in my name, will bring all things to your remembrance of everything I taught you (while he was with them in physical form). (John (Yahuchanon) 14:26) That's why it's important to obtain and possess the Ruach in our lives as a guide to the teachings of our Messiah through the obedience of faith.

And as earlier noted, many of the patriarchs and people struggled mightily (as many do to this present day) with this teaching because it requires more faith and obedience to the Spirit than objects on garments, head wraps, and beards, to name a few.

Bringing to an end the Levitical practices noted in the Law of Moses in exchange for the Laws and tenets of faith through obedience was the greatest accusation held against all those (Hebrew Israelites) who having accepted the teachings of the Messiah, after being converted (in which a lot of our people are not), and possessed the Ruach HaKodesh as required.

To wit, there are absolutely no teachings by the Messiah found that grants the freedom to forsake, ignore, and renounce the laws given to Moses by YAH himself. And as a reminder, not all commandments (the so-called 613) were etched in stone and given by YAH to Moses on the set-apart mountain. Laws were created by permission and introduced by Moses as the circumstances of our people changed, as noted earlier in the case of divorce.)

However, there were other laws that were given by YAH to Moses that only served as patterns, types, and shadows of greater things to come and have came. But there are too many of our people who are stuck on the old blueprints, prototypes, and models of the past and not conforming to its ultimate meaning – the actual representation (our Messiah) who was slain before the foundations of the world.

Also, every story you read in the book of Acts occurred during this war between Moses versus the Messiah in the eyes of many Hebrews; but for those who possess the Spirit, it was from Moses to the Messiah.

Even the disciple Stephen (Hebrew), who our writings describe as being "full of the Spirit" (Acts 6:5) suffered death for this very same reason found in Acts 6 at the hands of other Hebrews led by Paul (prior to his conversion).

**"Stephen, a man full of YAH's grace and power, performed amazing miracles and signs among the people. But one day some men from the Synagogue of Freed Slaves, as it was called, started to debate with him.**

They were Jews from Cyrene, Alexandria, Cilicia, and the province of Asia. None of them could stand against the wisdom and the Spirit with which Stephen spoke.

**So they persuaded some men to lie about Stephen, saying, 'We heard him blaspheme Moses, and even YAH.'**

**This roused the people, the elders, and the teachers of religious law. So they arrested Stephen and brought him before the high council.**

The lying witnesses said, 'This man is always speaking against the holy Temple and AGAINST THE LAWS OF MOSES. We have heard him say that this Messiah of Nazareth will destroy the Temple and **CHANGE THE CUSTOMS MOSES HANDED DOWN TO US**.'

**At this point everyone in the high council stared at Stephen, because his face became as bright as an angel's."** Acts (Ma'aseh) 6:8-15

See, because a lot of our people rejected the Messiah (either by way of unbelieving or disobedience, as it is this day) and viewed the teachings of the Messiah as an "Act of War" against the Laws of Moses and the customs Moses handed down.

And as earlier noted in the passage of Scripture, the "Synagogue of Freed Slaves," who were JEWS living in other lands (which reminds me about the modern-day street camps, as do the Pharisees and an abundance of religious leaders in that day, as well as the present day), was just one of the many groups that opposed any teaching related to the Messiah – especially related to the Law of Faith through obedience.

And just to note: this is NOT a Christian doctrine!!! Many Christians outright reject the Laws of Moses and are absolutely disobedient to the Words of our **HaMaschiach** while not truly embracing and understanding the ordinances of faith. Rather, many Christians (not all) live by the ways of man led by the "Spirit of Error" and not led by the "Spirit of Truth" unto obedience. (1 John (Yahuchanon) 4:6)

> "Then the high priest asked Stephen, "Are these accusations true?" This was Stephen's reply: "Brothers and fathers, listen to me." Acts (Ma'aseh) 7:1-2

I just wanted to reiterate the audience to whom Stephen was responding: men of his own Nation (Israel). Then Stephen, being led by the Ruach, began to speak and respond, beginning with the conversation from our patriarch Abraham through the history of many of our ancestors, and leading up to the present moment in time.

And through Stephen's speech and teachings to his kindred – the accusations against him teaching against the Laws of Moses and changing the customs handed down – were no longer at issue. The real issue was these powerful words spoken by Stephen:

> "You stiff-necked people with uncircumcised hearts and ears! You always resist the Ruach HaKodesh, just as your fathers did. Which of the prophets did your fathers fail to persecute?

> They even killed those (the prophets) who foretold the coming of the Righteous One. And now you are His betrayers and murderers

**– you who have received the law ordained by angels, yet have not kept it."** Acts (Ma'aseh) 7: 51-53

And why did Stephen tell these hypocrites that "you who have received the law yet have not kept it"? It was also noted later by Paul.

**"Now that no one is justified by the Law before YAH is evident; for, 'THE RIGHTEOUS MAN SHALL LIVE BY FAITH.'**

**However, the Law is not of faith; on the contrary, 'HE WHO PRACTICES THEM ARE REQUIRED TO LIVE BY THEM ALL (including all of its customs).'"** Galatians (Galatiym) 3:12

And you will always have Hebrews who are not led by the Spirit of YAH disobeying the Ruach HaKodesh. This is the answer to the thoughts of many modern-day "scattered" Israelites when it is said: "Why are we so in opposition of one another; why is there so much confusion amongst our people?"

And here's the answer in a nutshell, as earlier noted:

"…Now if any man have not the Spirit of the Messiah, he does not belong to him. And if Messiah be in you, the body is dead because of sin; but the Spirit is life because of righteousness.

For as many as are led by the Spirit of YAH, they are the sons (or children) of YAH." Romans (Romaiym) 8:9-14

"For not all who are descended from Israel are Israel." Romans (Romaiym) 9:6

In closing, the Ruach HaKodesh is promised to all those who fully obey YAH through the acceptance and message of truth through the Messiah.

The set-apart Spirit also serves as a seal, mark, or brand (similar to the blood that was smeared on the sides and tops of the doorframes of the houses in Egypt as a sign to the death angel to pass over and spare the life of the firstborn child).

Finally, the Ruach is the sealing of the oath and guarantee of our inheritance until the redemption of those who are YAH's possession are received to the praise of His glory.

"In Him we were also chosen as YAH's own, having been predestined according to the plan of Him who works out everything by the counsel of His will in order that we, who were the first to hope in Messiah, would be for the praise of His glory.

And in Him, having heard and believed the word of truth – the gospel of your salvation (restoration) – you were sealed with the promised Ruach HaKodesh, who is the pledge of our inheritance until the redemption of those who are YAH's possession, to the praise of His glory." Ephesians (Eph'siym) 1:9-14.

"...and he has identified us as his own by placing the Holy Spirit (Ruach) in our hearts as the first installment that guarantees everything he has promised us." 2 Corinthians (Qorintiym) 1:22. (See also 2 Corinthians 5:1-5.)

In Luke (Lucas) 9, it tells us that when Peter woke up the next morning after an extensive day of ministry, he witnessed the glory of the Messiah (the YAH's splendor and grandeur resonating on his Son). But Peter also recognized and identified two other interesting figures in conversation with the HaMaschiach: Elijah and Moses.

When Peter saw these great men with the Messiah, he did something most of us would have done and what most of us are doing now. The passage of Scripture affirms that as these figures of Elijah and Moses (both were precursors that led the way to the Messiah) were departing the scene, Peter stated, "Let me make THREE booths" or "three shelters as memorials."

**Please Note:** In the days of the Messiah, it was John the Baptist who was noted as coming in the "spirit of Elijah," who was a forerunner to the coming of the Messiah. John the Baptist was the end of the Levitical priesthood, being from the tribe of Levi – and the HaMaschiach, being from the tribe of Judah, was the beginning of the new priesthood:

I've often asked myself, now why would Peter be so eager to build three shelters as memorials, knowing these figures cannot remain there? But as I read more about the purposes of booths, it broadened my knowledge. Booths were a temporary shelter, usually made of shrubs and tree branches, used to PROTECT cattle against the weather and to serve as a mark of respect to them.

So, we can conclude that when Peter made this statement, he was aiming to protect those whom he strongly admired. In creating monumental tributes to honor such esteemed men, Peter would be reminded every time he passed by the mountains and saw these booths that he was in the company of great men. In fact, no implications in the Scriptures leads us to believe that he even thought about making himself a booth, or making a booth for James and John, who were with him, but he offered to make these great men of YAH booths of memorials.

Now, please observe with me this point! Peter didn't just offer to make the Messiah a booth, but also booths for Elijah and Moses as well. Peter included the Messiah, but he also included Elijah and Moses on the **same pedestal** with the Messiah. Elijah and Moses were great men of YAH who accomplished many remarkable things, so it was quite natural for Peter to include these men with the Messiah.

Peter did not exclude the Messiah but included him, which tells us that Peter had great love and respect for the Son of YAH, just as much as he had for Elijah and Moses.

However, no matter what the case may have been, please notice how YAH responded to what Peter was thinking and had spoken. Luke 9:34 goes on to say that as Peter was observing these great men of faith standing with the Messiah, and communicating his thoughts about the things he would like to do for them, a cloud came down and overshadowed them (Peter, James, and John). They were overtaken with terror and stunned with fear as they entered into the cloud.

Simultaneously, as Peter was saying "let's do something" for these great men of YAH, the cloud came and *impaired his vision*. Peter, James, and John could no longer see these men of YAH. Because of the intensity and thickness of the cloud, their vision was impaired, meaning their focus was blurred, distorted, and imprecise.

YAH did not wait until after Peter completed building the booths for the Messiah, Elijah, and Moses, neither did YAH wait until after Peter was finished sharing his thoughts (because of his influence and the impact he had on the others around him, such as James and John). They were fearful because they could not see.

Look what happened in Luke 9:35. As Peter, James, and John were frightened by the cloud, they heard a distinctive and clear voice, which expressed to them:

"THIS IS MY SON (the Messiah), my dearly beloved; HEAR HIM ONLY – the one that I elected and preferred. Pay attention to and surrender to him with your full obedience."

Then, when the cloud cleared and the voice faded away, Peter, James, and John looked up and saw the Messiah and the Messiah ONLY, for he was standing there ALONE.

YAH will not share His glory with another man or woman, whether they are striving to do good or evil.

In the times beforehand, the hope and salvation for Israel was governed by the laws, writings, and prophets to the coming of the Messiah, but in these last days we must pay strict attention to the Messiah and heed him:

"In the past YAH spoke to our ancestors through the prophets at many times and in various ways, but in these last days he has spoken to us by his Son, whom he appointed heir of all things, and through whom also he made the universe." Hebrews (Ivriym) 1:1-2

# 3
# FREE BUT YET BOUND

IN this period in which "Awakened Israel" is becoming more and more conscious of their elected heritage by the Spirit of the Most High, I often liken this phenomenal event to the story of the HaMaschiach and Lazarus found in John (Yahuchanon) 11. Here, the children of Israel, throughout each passing generation and presently, metaphorically represents Lazarus in this entire chapter, from beginning to end.

> **G2976 - *Lazaros***
> **Outline of Biblical Usage:**
> I. Lazarus = "whom God helps" (a form of the Hebrew name Eleazar)
>   A. an inhabitant of Bethany, beloved by Christ and raised from the dead by him
>   B. a very poor and wretched person to whom Jesus referred to in Luke 16:20-25

The story begins by describing the condition of Lazarus in which he was "sick." Interestingly enough, the name Lazarus from (G2976) means: "Whom YAH helps." The story continues by showing how Lazarus's relatives and kinsmen pleaded to our Messiah for healing and restoration for the state of his current condition. Many of our patriarchs have done so throughout each transitory generation, both prayed and supplicated, for the well-being and health of Israel: from Moses to Deborah; from Solomon to Elijah and Paul (Numbers 21:7; Judges 4-5; 1 Kings 8:28-30; Romans 10:1; Romans 11:2-3).

And as noted in the story, the Messiah's response to all those who entreated for Lazarus (and Israel) was this: Lazarus's (and Israel's) sickness will not end or continue in death, but will be raised up from the dead so that YAH will be glorified.

**"But the YAH will save the people of Israel with eternal salvation. Throughout everlasting ages, they will never again be humiliated and disgraced."** Isaiah (Yesha'yahu) 45:17

Although YAH made a promise that ultimately, in the end, the people of Israel will never be humiliated and disgraced again, as noted in Isaiah 45:17 and summed up in John 11, YAH (through the Messiah) is purposely tarrying and has not fully completed this promise yet. And because He is prolonging his coming, more and more of us (as a whole) are growing impatient and becoming stagnated in our relationship with Him and in the hope of his return, as evidently noted in the way that we behave and live in this present world. And it is important that we be reminded of this:

**"For the grace of YAH has been revealed, bringing salvation to all (his) people. And we are instructed to turn from godless living and sinful pleasures.**

We should live in this evil world with wisdom, righteousness, and devotion to YAH, while we look forward with hope to that wonderful day when the glory of our great Messiah will be revealed.

**He gave his life to free us from every kind of sin, to cleanse us, and to make us his very own people, totally committed to doing good deeds."** Titus (Titos) 2:11-14

We have to understand, as the Messiah is purposely tarrying in his return in restoration of his people, Israel, the Scripture tells us that this salvation, this restoration of hope which has come to those who are spiritually awakened, is supposed to instruct and teach us something while we are patiently waiting for his return.

So, what is the lesson? What is this salvation supposed to teach us? It is supposed to teach us (while we're waiting) that we MUST turn away from empty and vain living (the standards we have been taught by those who rule over us), along with SINFUL pleasures (pleasures that transgress the ways of YAH) in this PRESENT AGE. We have to strive to live a set-apart life (through his Spirit). NOW, not only after he returns, but prior to his return.

Again, this is NOT saying that you can't have pleasurable moments in this life, but you're not supposed to take part in VAIN and EMPTY LIVING and *SINFUL* PLEASURES.

In addition, for this salvation he admonishes his people to live in this evil world with wisdom, righteousness, and commitment to YAH before we can even look forward with hope to that wonderful day of his return.

As we continue in the book of John (Yahuchanon) 11, the Messiah finally arrives on the scene to awaken Lazarus out of what the Messiah called "A Deep Sleep" and "Death." Sad but true, this deep sleep and death is permanent to the majority of our people as the Scriptures foretell, but to the remnant of Israel (and as shown with Lazarus), this deep sleep and spiritual death is temporal.

And as we approach verse 43 to get to the main point of discussion, I would like to point out that throughout this entire story, you will always have unbelieving and doubting Hebrews (and people in general) along the way making statements of disbelief regarding the message/sayings given to us by our Messiah (while he's tarrying), as well as other believing Hebrews who walk/live more by sight than by faith. 2 Corinthians 5:17

As our HaMaschiach shouts to Israel through his word and spirit as he shouted to Lazarus to "come forth" and to "come out" of this deep sleep and spiritual death, many of us have awakened to his cry and call. And then for many of us – **it ends there** – with just knowing "We Are Israel." With many of us we are simply satisfied with knowing that "We Are a Special People."

But something of significance happened immediately after Lazarus (Israel) had awakened and come forth from his state of deep sleep and/or death. The Scripture goes on to state that his "hands and feet" were still BOUND in grave clothes and his "head" continued to be BOUND with a "head cloth" and/or "napkin (handkerchief)." From that I give the title "FREE BUT YET BOUND."

The lexical from G2750 states that the *"grave clothes,"* mentioned regarding Lazarus's hands/feet being bound also, are used when binding a corpse after it has been swathed in linen; and the *Strong's* definition states that it also represents "an uncertain affinity or resemblance," meaning you become unrecognizable under all the grave clothes.

> ### G2750 - *keiria*
> **Outline of Biblical Usage:**
> I. a band, either for bed-girth, or for tying up a corpse after it has been swathed in linen

Furthermore, the lexical from G4676 states that the *"head cloth, napkin, and/or handkerchief"* that's mentioned regarding Lazarus's face remaining bound are used when swathing (or binding) the head of a corpse. And although by definition this term can also be used for wiping off sweat and perspiration, in this context it is referring to a cloth that binds the head that's used during burial. We know that a dead person cannot perspire or sweat.

> **G4676 - *soudarion***
>
> **Strong's Definitions:** σουδάριον soudárion, soo-dar'-ee-on; of Latin origin; a sudarium (sweat-cloth), i.e. towel (for wiping the perspiration from the face, or binding the face of a corpse):— handkerchief, napkin.

In continuing the story, the Messiah was NOT satisfied simply because Lazarus (Israel) arose from his deep sleep/death. He commanded that he (or we) be freed from the bondage of grave clothes and head cloths, which represented death or dead things.

**"Stand fast therefore in the liberty wherewith the Messiah hath made us free and be not entangled again with the yoke of bondage."** Galatians (Galatiym) 5:1 (KJV)

We who are truly awakened (and not just with knowledge or with the amount of information that a person may obtain) and have been summoned from our spiritual death MUST allow the Most High through the Messiah to free us from the dead works or the fruitless way of living we once lived in and abided by when we were dead in our trespasses and sin. Our lives MUST no longer represent the dead (works) but the living.

"If you then be risen with the HaMaschiach, seek those things which are above, where the Messiah sits on the right hand of YAH.

Set your affections on things above and not on things on the earth. For you (your old man/woman – your old way of living and behaving) are dead and your life is hid with the Messiah in YAH.

Then, when our Messiah, who is our life, appears then shall you also appear with him in glory." Colossians (Qolasiym) 3:1-4 (KJV)

**Change for many does not happen overnight but through a process of time**; but conversion can and will only come <u>if we recognize the necessity for it</u> and the desire to be transformed into the image of our HaMaschiach.

# 4
# CHANGING THE WAY WE THINK

Our people, the true physical descendants of our ancestors Abraham, Isaac, and Jacob, have undergone an enormous transformation of culture and lifestyle from the former generations in comparison to those who live in this present age. Throughout each passing generation, the more our ancestors clung to the pagan deities and images of the surrounding nations, (especially during the periods of our enslavements and bondages), the more we abandoned our cultural way of living (as orchestrated by YAH) in exchange for the universal customs and practices of these heathen nations.

In my opinion, no other era has been more cultural damaging to the thinking process and behavior of our people than the Hellenization period of the Greeks, the Arab Sub-Saharan, and the Transatlantic Slave Trade. Although Israel went into captivity under Egypt, Assyria, and Babylon, etc., as well as in and out of captivity during the time of the Judges, a great number of our people still remembered who they were and who to cry out to in a time of desperation and extreme anxiety.

However, for many of us throughout time, as well as a vast number of our ancestors who preceded us, reluctantly fell into the category of this Scripture passage perfectly:

**"...And there arose another generation after them, which knew not YAH, nor yet the works of YAH which he had done for Israel aforetime."** Judges (Shofetiym) 2:10

Also, as prophesied by our earlier prophets because of our disobedience to the Most High:

**"And thou, even thyself, shall discontinue from thine heritage that I gave thee; and I will cause thee to serve thine enemies in the land which thou knowest not: for you have kindled a fire in mine anger, which shall burn for ever."** Jeremiah (Yirmeyahu) 17:4 (KJV

And this is one of the main reasons why the so-called "Blacks and Negroes" don't remember who they are. All we remember is what we are being taught by our parents, as well as the current traditions of the society in which we reside. We have no former remembrance of our rich inheritance because it has been (temporarily) discontinued.

# Hellenization Period of Israel

This is a transcript taken from one of my previous books entitled *Leaving Christianity*, written by me and a great brother and colleague, Casey Clark. From page 55, regarding this dreadful period of Israel where a large percentage of our people volunteered, and others were forced, to abandon our way of life in exchange for the customs of the Greeks.

"Hellenism is usually associated with the fusion of Greek and non-Greek culture. It is also defined as the adoption of Greek thought, customs, and lifestyles covering the period from Alexander the Great to the beginnings of the Roman Empire. The term carries a much broader meaning in biblical scholarship, being closely synonymous with the term Greco-Roman.

"Alexander and his successors, notably Antipater, Perdiccas, Ptolemy I, Seleucus I, Antigonus I, and Lysimachus, dismantled political, cultural, and religious establishments, while introducing their culture with the progressive spread of the Greek language. Hellenistic conquest subsequently altered every nation they subdued, including the House of Israel. The influence of Greek ideology, culture, and religion could not be totally prevented after the Seleucid empire gained sovereignty of Palestine in 198 B.C.

"The Hebrew people came under intense and severe pressure to Hellenize and, as a result of this, many rebelled, igniting the Maccabean War beginning in 168 B.C.E. Hellenism's strong hold was most prominent among Hebrews of the dispersion, primarily in Alexandria, Egypt, which is by no coincidence the place of origin of the Hebrew-to-Greek translation called the Septuagint. This first translation of the Scriptures took place about 275 B.C.E.

"This need for a Greek translation came about as a result of Yisraelites (Israelites) who spoke only Greek and no longer spoke their native tongue. A Hellenized Hebrew by the name of Philo (30 B.C.E.-A.D. 40) re-explained their beliefs and practices, making them compatible or in agreement with Greek philosophy. Unfortunately, this was another consequence resulting from the spread and adoption of Hellenism, which in my opinion gave rise to a more Greek-centered form of worship and culture, subsequently leaving behind the sacredness that set the Hebrew people apart from their Gentile neighbors.

It is also difficult for me to believe that they would not be more willing to take on a more Hellenistic form of the Most High's name as another way to assimilate and not to draw attention.

**Hellenism Breeds Apostasy**

During the early decades of Seleucide rule, many Yisraelites (Israelites) were free to worship as they chose, at least until the days of Antiochus IV (175-163 B.C.E.). The desire to bring his kingdom into unification led Antiochus IV to forcefully impose Greek beliefs on the House of Yisrael (Israel), along with other conquered peoples.

Regrettably, numerous wicked Yisraelites were eager and willing to embrace all things Greek. Ambitious and Hellenistic-minded Hebrews competed for the appointment of the high priest position that was chosen by the Seleucid kings.

"In those days went there out of Israel wicked men, who persuaded many saying, "Let us go and make a covenant with 'the heathen' that are round about us: for since we departed from them we have had much sorrow. So this device (plan) pleased them well.

**Then certain of the people were so forward (zealous) herein, that they went to the king; who gave them license to do after the ordinances of the heathen.**

Wherein they built a place of exercise (Coliseum – a form of pagan entertainment) at Jerusalem according to the "customs of the heathen.

**And made themselves uncircumcised, and forsook the holy covenant, and joined themselves to the heathen, and were sold to do mischief."** 1 Maccabees 1:11-15

The traditionalistic Hebrew followers of the Torah found the embracing of Hellenism to be in opposition and began to organize themselves under the name Hasidim (the devout). This movement grew and would later give rise to the sect of the Pharisees.

Antiochus IV thought to dismantle the Hebrew belief system and their culture surrounding it. He attributed the root of their resistance with their religion and made the compliance of Sabbath-keeping, circumcision, possession of the Torah, and the keeping of its observances prohibited. If caught, one would be executed. This vile, idolatrous Greek king took it upon himself to pervert the temple by dedicating it to his deity Zeus and offering a sacrificial offering of swine upon its altar.

Apparently, this was a dark time for many in Yisrael and to think that their very lives were at stake for doing what was not only their belief but everyday practices! At the time of this writing, I am living in America, but what if practices of everyday life, such as visiting friends and family, attending worship, reading the Scriptures within your own home, praying publically, and anything that remotely appeared to reflect the righteousness of the Most High to a pagan-controlled government, was punishable by death, what would many of us do?

Some of us have young children, wives, husbands, close friends, and family members we care for deeply, and yet all could be in danger of death because of what you or I choose not only to believe but by what method that belief is acted upon! Here is an insert giving more detail of this dark time period from the Book of 1 Maccabees 1:41-51:

**"Then the king wrote to his whole kingdom that all should be ONE PEOPLE, and that each should give up his customs. All the Gentiles accepted the command of the king.**

Many even from Israel gladly adopted his religion; they sacrificed to idols and profaned the Sabbath.

And the king sent letters by messengers to Jerusalem and the cities of Judah; he directed them to follow customs strange to the land, to forbid burnt offerings and sacrifices and drink offerings in the sanctuary, to profane Sabbaths and feasts, to defile the sanctuary and the priests, to build altars and sacred precincts and shrines for idols, to sacrifice swine and unclean animals, and to leave their sons uncircumcised.

They were to make themselves abominable by everything unclean and profane, so that they should forget the law and change all the ordinances. And whoever does not obey the command of the king shall die.

In such words he wrote to his whole kingdom. And he appointed inspectors over all the people and commanded the cities of Judah to offer sacrifice, city by city. Many of the people, everyone who forsook the law, joined them, and they did evil in the land."

And these abominable practices have not only been entangled in the framework of many of our ancestors before us, generation after generation; but today, many heathenistic cultures and practices sit at the root and core of our mental conditioning.

So, at the time of the Messiah, there stood different factions of our people Israel. You had Judeans (so-called Jews), who (some but not all) were a bulk of those from the Southern Tribe, although (some) were not touched by the influence of Hellenism – many were solely entangled with self-righteousness through the works of law.

Then you have some of our people from the Northern Tribes, who were not altogether converted to Greek customs; however, many followed the ways of the ruling nations that resided over us, from generation to generation, as well as some who followed various aspects or forms of our Hebrew traditions.

Then you had the majority (not all) of remainder of Israel (also called Greeks, Grecians, and Gentiles) throughout the New Testament writings.

For example: as noted earlier and repeated for edification purposes:

**"And in those days, when the number of the disciples was multiplied, there arose a murmuring of the Grecians against the**

Hebrews, because their widows were neglected in the daily ministration." Acts (Ma'aseh) 6:1

Again: Grecian: from a derivative of G1672: a Hellenist or Greek-speaking Jew – Grecian.

A Hellenist: one who imitates the manners and customs or the worship of the Greeks, and use the Greek tongue.

Used in the NT of Jews born in foreign lands and speaking Greek – *Strong's NT 1675.*

One who copies the manners and worship of the Greeks or who use the Greek language, a Hellenist, i.e., one who imitates the manners and customs or the worship of the Greeks, and uses the Greek tongue; employed in the NT of Jews born in foreign lands and speaking Greek (Grecian Jews).

And this was presented before that took place in Israel during the Hellenistic period of Greeks for the duration of the Maccabean Era:

So, when the Messiah came on the scene, many of our people were called Gentiles, Greeks, and Grecians, mainly because many of our ancestors imitated the manners and customs or the worship of the Greeks, and used the Greek tongue/language.

And this is still our main struggle today. Many of our people do not remember their rich heritage as Israelites. Because we have adopted and imitate the manners and customs or the worship of the American way (or whatever country you have been customized in), and use the English language or the dialect of our oppressors, and not your own unpolluted, pure Hebrew tongue. And why did I say **unpolluted?** Because the Hebrew language as known in the present day is not the original dialect and has even been tainted by our oppressors.

And this is the speech and mindset (and the heart of this chapter) when the apostle Paul made this statement to his people – who were strongly influenced by the customs of the Gentiles.

**"And so, dear brothers and sisters, I plead with you to give your bodies to YAH because of all he has done for you. Let them be a living and holy sacrifice – the kind he will find acceptable. This is truly the way to worship him.**

**And be not confirmed or don't copy the behavior and customs of this world (the present age), but let YAH transform you into a new person by CHANGING THE WAY YOU THINK. Then you will learn to know YAH's will for you, which is good and pleasing and perfect."** Romans (Romaiym) 12:1-2 (NLT)

And before I go into the context of this passage, let's look into rightly dividing the meaning to understand the audience to which this message was being broadcast. Christianity and other forms of religion have misappropriated the proper context of Scripture by having everyone believe that Paul's messages, as well as the messages of many other letters and writings, were spoken in a general context for whosoever and whatsoever. However, the last time Paul used the terms "brethren" or "brothers and sisters," he made it quite clear to whom he was speaking:

**"For I could wish that I myself were accursed from the Messiah for my brethren, my countrymen according to the flesh."** Romans (Romaiym) 9:3

And, as you observe the book of Romans 12:1-2, what is the thesis of the subject matter? Sacrifice. Because aforetime this was a requirement and custom for the Hebrews to perform for the atonement of sin and for celebration offerings. In addition, it was the Hebrews who were given a separate standard of living contrary to the way the world (or other nations) lived.

Now that we've cleared up the intended audience, let's understand the emphasis of the passage at hand. Paul not only highlighted (once we become aware of our true identity) that we must become a living sacrifice to YAH (in terms of him using us to the point of death or, i.e., death to our own personal agendas and careers, etc.), but a sacrifice that He finds to be good and pleasing in his own sight.

The book of Proverbs (Mishlei) states in 14:12, and again in 16:25:

**"There is a way which seems right unto a man, but the end thereof are the ways of death."**

If mankind cannot truly create life then how can they create their own path in life? Moreover, the right path in life? For mankind can reproduce but cannot create human life (and artificial intelligence are NOT humans).

But, in order to successfully complete this task (becoming a living sacrifice for YAH), we must not **COPY THE BEHAVIOR AND CUSTOMS OF THE WORLD**, and those of us (which is most of us) who have already been programmed by the customs of this world, must allow YAH to transform us into a new person by **CHANGING THE WAY WE THINK.**

The Father desires to take us back to the way he previously programmed His people to think and live because we have fallen so deep into despair, hopelessness, and depression in the absence of his identity.

We have been systematically controlled and deceived into believing what I call "the illusion of inclusion" to keep us off track and preoccupied with fantasies, false impressions, and dreams of temporal success. We have been tossed to and fro by every wind of doctrine (the variety of belief systems and teachings) by the sleight of hand and cunning craftiness of men, whereby they lie in wait to deceive (with lies and deceptions so clever they will sound like the truth). Ephesians (Eph'siym) 4:14

We are last in every poll, in every economic funding, and in practically everything. As a people, we have been told that it's our fault that we are this way because we are lazy and incapable of achieving. And when we attempt success, such as Black Wall Street, one of the most prominent concentrations of the so-called African American businesses in the United States during the early 20th century (until the Tulsa race riot of 1921), this history is erased from human minds and is not taught as an influential part of American history.

During that time, white residents massacred hundreds of black residents and annihilated their neighborhoods within hours. The riot was one of the most devastating massacres in the history of U.S. race relations, completely obliterating the once-thriving Greenwood communities.

This shows us only one thing: When we as a people attempt to get ahead, this system is designed to keep us defeated as a people. And those who appear to have figured it out are just billboards or models for the rich, wealthy, and the elitist, to be used like puppets or slaves.

When Marcus Garvey attempted to figure it out and unify us with our own businesses, etc., he was undermined in defeat. The same story repeats over and over again with many influential leaders. In similar fashion, I've observed the same attempts from current leaders in establishing black-owned banks, black-owned businesses, etc. These attempts are not new, but are cycled by each passing generation. It is possible to accomplish; however, they too, will be undermined in some form and fashion, some type of destruction from outside forces. (They may even use a "black face" as a scapegoat to accomplish their devious plans.) I applaud the black leaders and brothers and sisters for their attempts, but to what end while we are still oppressed in this country and are continually counted as sheep for the slaughter?

Our true solution and deliverance as a people is to permanently turn back to YAH and gain the wisdom and knowledge needed from him to proceed in life as "foreigners and strangers" in this Babylonian system of oppression.

This reminds me of a story of our people found in 2 Chronicles (Hayamiym) 20.

When the enemy encamped about our people to destroy us, the text states that ALL Judah and the inhabitants of Jerusalem, including the KING and leaders, prayed that YAH would deliver them, prayed for his power and might, acknowledged that they were fearful and afraid, and reminded themselves of their covenant and promises. I love the fact that King Jehoshaphat made this beautiful statement:

"Oh YAH, won't you stop them? We are powerless against this mighty army that is about to attack us. We do not know what to do, but we are looking to you for help." (NLT)

And again:

"Oh YAH our Elohim, wilt thou not judge them? For we have no might against this great company that cometh against us; neither know we what to do: but our eyes are upon thee." (KJV)

And, as the story continues, when the people of YAH unified collectively and acknowledged their inability to defeat such a great enemy, our Father responded with, **"This battle is not yours; but mine and I will defeat this mighty enemy that threatened your cause."**

And this is the only way this great depression that plagues our people will be defeated, turning collectively as one people, returning permanently back to YAH. For he is the only one who can break this seemingly endless cycle of curses that our people do currently occupy.

Our state of condition as a whole will NOT change because of a vote, will not change because of who we "think" we select as the President of the United States. (Because, after all, presidents are not elected but selected by the elite majority, and the rest of society is deceived through the process of voting and elections. When you think about it, not ONE electronic or manual vote can be realistically verified and counted.)

And it is an unfortunate evil that our people have been groomed to believe that we matter or count as an equal citizen of society. We are but like cattle, and our gifts, talents, and creativity are prostituted for great wealth in the sight of the elitist (the rich and wealthy) five (5) percent of the entire population who temporarily have a stranglehold on the governing bodies of the world (i.e., banks, government, legislation, military, land, TV, entertainment, etc.)

And for this very reason our Father provokes his people not to copy the behavior and customs of the world and that we have to be changed, starting with the way we have been groomed to think. After all, if the world hates the righteous way of our Messiah, and you claim to be a follower of the Messiah, how then can the world love and **embrace you**?

**"If the world hates you, remember that it hated me first. The world would love you as one of its own if you belonged to it, but you are no longer part of the world. I chose you to come out of the world, so it hates you."** John (Yahuchanon) 15:18-19

Again, YAH gave us the enlightenment of our true identity as the descendants of Hebrews and chose us to come out of the world; we should not remain eagerly occupied by its nature.

Now let's be clear on what the word "world' means because it holds three distinct meanings:

- **Aion:** an age, generation, or period marked by time.
- **Oikoumene:** the physical land mass or the inhabited earth.
- **Kosmos:** governmental order of arrangement for the human race or the present systematic condition of human affairs in alienation from and is in opposition against anything that pertains to the righteousness of YAH. This can also mean the order of arrangement for the Nation of Israel.

And in the majority of Scripture passages when the word **world** is used, it is specifically linked to **Kosmos**. As the Messiah stated, **"Although we are in the world (kosmos); we are not supposed to**

**be of this world."** (Or governed by the systematic condition of human affairs that are designed to be in complete opposition to YAH.)

Time after time as we read and meditate upon biblical texts, you'll often see and hear many passages that repeatedly admonish us to **"Come out from among her** (the worldly system of society) **or come from among them** (unbelievers and their idols) **and separate entirely says YAH and touch not the unclean** (or immoral) **thing; then I will receive and welcome you as a Father over many sons and daughters."** (2 Corinthians 6:16-18)

And again, we are in this world but should not be linked to anything in opposition to YAH.

Essentially, this is our crossroads (so to speak). This is our kryptonite – disassociating ourselves from the manners and/or practices of this present world and striving to cleave to the ways of the Most High YAH.

Letting go of this wicked voting system, worldly politics, the celebrations of pagan holidays, the deception of worldly entertainment (just to name a few) and the many customs that have been purposely designed to keep our people captivated in deceit, while remaining clueless about who we really are simultaneously keeps us believing and hoping that true changes for our people will come through this Americanized, adopted, wicked Babylonian system (in which many countries share alike).

We need to allow YAH, second by second, moment by moment, day by day to change the way we think and behave. This passage of Scripture tells us this:

**"Since you have been raised to new life with Messiah, set your sights on the realities of heaven, where Messiah sits in the place of honor at YAH's right hand.**

Think about the things of heaven, not the things of earth. For you died to this life, and your real life is hidden with the Messiah in YAH.

**And when the Messiah, who is your (real) life, is revealed to the whole world, you will share in all his glory.**

So put to death the sinful, earthly things lurking within you. Have nothing to do with sexual immorality, impurity, lust, and evil desires. Don't be greedy, for a greedy person is an idolater, worshiping the things of this world.

**Because of these sins, the anger of YAH is coming."** Colossians (Qolasiym) 3:1-6

We must learn to be willing to let go of the customs of this present world and society in order to embrace and received the true riches of YAH.

# 5
# A PREPARED PEOPLE FOR A PREPARED PLACE

There is a thought "out there" floating in Hebrew-land amongst Israelites that all you have to do in order to be ready for the return of our Messiah (for those who actually believe in the Messiah) is follow some laws, honor the Sabbath, wear your tassels and head wraps, while warning our women not to wear pants – but this couldn't be farther than the truth.

We will truly look into why this passage of Scripture echoes and the meaning behind it:

"And she shall bring forth a son, and thou shalt call his name (YAHAWASHI/YASHUA): for he shall save his people from their sins." Matthew (Mattithyahu) 1:21

Let's focus on two important aspects of this Scripture: save –from their sins.

*Saved (from G4982):* sozo: meaning to keep safe and sound, to rescue from danger or destruction. To save a suffering one from perishing; to restore to health. In addition to be delivered from the penalties of the Messianic judgment.

---

### G4982 - *sōzō*

**Outline of Biblical Usage:**

*I.* to save, keep safe and sound, to rescue from danger or destruction

   *A.* one (from injury or peril)

      *i.* to save a suffering one (from perishing), i.e. one suffering from disease, to make well, heal, restore to health

      *ii.* to preserve one who is in danger of destruction, to save or rescue

   *B.* to save in the technical biblical sense

      *i.* negatively

         *a.* to deliver from the penalties of the Messianic judgment

         *b.* to save from the evils which obstruct the reception of the Messianic deliverance

---

Sins (from G266): hamartea: meaning to wander from the law of YAH, to violate YAH's law: to sin. That which is done wrong, an offence, a violation of the Divine law in thought or in action.

### G266 - *hamartia*

**Outline of Biblical Usage:**

I. equivalent to 264

    A. to be without a share in

    B. to miss the mark

    C. to err, be mistaken

    D. to miss or wander from the path of uprightness and honour, to do or go wrong

    E. to wander from the law of God, violate God's law, sin

II. that which is done wrong, sin, an offence, a violation of the divine law in thought or in act

III. collectively, the complex or aggregate of sins committed either by a single person or by many

Now apart from misinformed teachings and partial beliefs: again as a refresher, what are YAH's Divine Laws:

Deuteronomy (Devariym) 8:1-3:

"And he humbled thee, and suffered thee to hunger, and fed thee with manna, which thou knewest not, neither did thy fathers know; that he might make thee know that man doth not live by bread only, but by EVERY word that proceedeth out of the mouth of YAH doth man live." (KJV)

So, in essence, one of the many purposes for our Messiah coming was to rescue Israel and deliver us from the penalties of the Messianic judgment from violation of the Divine law (every word given to us by YAH) in "thought or in actions."

Now how could this be truly accomplished simply by me instructing you that – "You are an Israelite: keep YAH's commandments, don't shave your beards, wear your tassels, keep the Sabbath day and feast days, and women don't wear pants."

For me, it's absurd to even think it's that simple, and those whose message resembles those statements as noted above usually fail to mention that we can only be restored by our continual obedience to YAH through his Son, not by our OWN POWER OR MIGHT, but by YAH's spirit and HIS Spirit alone. Zechariah (Zakaryahu) 4:6

Many of us also fail to keep this engraved in our souls:

**"Whosoever denieth the Son (Messiah), the same hath NOT the Father (YAH): (but) he that acknowledgeth the Son hath the Father also."** 1 John (Yahuchanon) 2:23

And the word "denial" is not solely a statement of some sort in acceptance or denial of the Messiah as much as it means from (G720): arneomi: meaning not to accept, to reject, to refuse something offered; as in many cases: the very words from/of our Messiah.

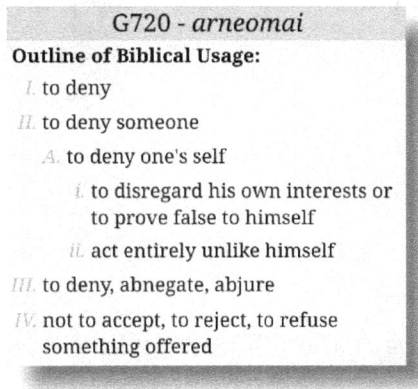

Salvation has many folds or variations in completion of the whole process which also includes one day we (our people as a whole) will be saved (or rescued) from under the power of our oppressors.

**"As he spake by the mouth of his holy prophets, which have been since the world began: That we should be saved from our enemies, and from the hand of all that hate us."** Luke (Lucas) 1:70-71

HalleluYAH!!! to that particular moment in time to come, but in the meantime and in-between time we must allow YAH through our

Messiah to prepare us, a people (set-apart as a bride for her groom) for a prepared place.

Our preparation as a people is necessary in order to receive our glorification in new bodies prior to the 1000-year reign on earth (in which we'll be gather in our own land; and cities rebuilt) prior to our final destination and permanent resting place in New Jerusalem.

Just being awakened to the fact that you are an Israelite is NOT ENOUGH. Ahab, was one of the Kings from our Northern Tribes, although he knew who he was, he was also desperately wicked and eventually was cut off from being one of the people.

Being saved from our sins, is a continual act of allowing the MOST HIGH to deliver us from beneath the POWER/CONTROL of SIN, which we have learned and inherited from our ancestors through the practices of heathens, which keeps/kept us bound in chains and shackled beneath the Law of Sin in resemblance to the everyday physical nature of the heathens and nations around us.

That's why we were often commanded to "Walk in the Light."

**"As long as I am in the world, I am the light of the world."** John (Yahuchanon) 9:5

"While ye have light, believe in the light, that ye may be the children of light. These things spake the Messiah, and departed, and did hide himself." John (Yahuchanon) 12:36

"But if we walk in the light, as he is in the light, we have fellowship one with another, and the blood of the Messiah cleanseth (continued process due to transgressions) us from ALL SIN." 1 John (Yahuchanon) 1:7

As noted in the earlier readings, although many of us now declare without a shadow of a doubt that we are the children of our ancestors – the Hebrews/Israelites – we must allow YAH to continue to deliver us from mimicking the behavior and practices of our enemies, and to reflect the behavior of our Messiah in "act" and "thought," – hence, walking in the Light.

"Dear children, let's not merely say that we love each other; let us show the truth by our actions. Our actions will show that we belong to the truth, so we will be confident when we stand before YAH." 1 John (Yahuchanon) 3:18-19 (NLT)

This is why the Messiah stated this in many places:

"But he that shall endure unto the end, the same shall be saved (rescued/restored)." Matthew (Mattithyahu) 24:13 (KJV)

With all of the hell that challenged our people to quit and give up (in pressing toward the mark and calling of The Most High) in acceptance and exchange for the ways, lifestyle, practices, and behaviors of the heathens and powers that be; through many forms of trials/persecutions, many may find it will be much easier to accept the nature of our enemies; consequently, no longer fighting the good fight of faith – laying hold on eternal life. 1 Timothy (Timotheus) 6:12

Again, this fight for Israel to be reestablished in the world to come isn't based on just a confession of faith, the outer works of the law, coupled with a change of garments, and a practice of feast days as holidays/holy days. This is about allowing the Almighty YAH to clean house inwardly within our spirit and souls: casting out demons and wicked spirits that made their homes within us; the worldly music from yesteryear that we continue to make excuses for, and in allowing those spirits in secular music to have their place in us.

And there are a plethora of other things I could have mentioned in the same light as music: the evil lusts and desires, the using our set-apart temples as "smoking houses" for the use of drugs, and so on and so forth, etc. We all fall short in some form and fashion. That's why we need to continue pressing toward acknowledging our insufficiencies in exchange for true deliverance and restoration of spiritual health in becoming **"The True Children of Israel – a Set-Apart People."**

"If we confess our sins, he is faithful and just to forgive us our sins, and to cleanse us from all unrighteousness. If we say that we have not sinned, we make him a liar, and his word is not in us." 1 John (Yahuchanon) 1:9-10

Confessing our sins and being forgiven of our sins are present-plural action verbs in which, regrettably, you will have those who confess the latter, that they have not sinned or do sin or transgress the righteousness ways of YAH in some form or fashion, which is unfortunate and to their shame.

But for those who acknowledge that the flesh is weak, albeit the spirit is willing, we have to allow his grace and salvation to continually teach us something – which requires action from us before we can truly claim the glory that will be revealed in us at his coming/return – as noted in earlier writings:

"For the grace of YAH that bringeth salvation hath appeared to all men, teaching us that, denying ungodliness and worldly lusts, we should live soberly, righteously, and godly, in this present world;

**Looking for that blessed hope, and the glorious appearing of the great elohim and our Saviour Yahawashi; who gave himself for us, that he might redeem us from ALL INIQUITY and purify unto himself a peculiar people, zealous of good works.**" Titus (Titos) 2:11-14

Now, this is how grace is supposed to work, not for us to continue in sin that his grace may abound or become null and void, but in the hope of being salvaged and fully restored to our place as YAH has foreordained before the foundations of the world and has appeared to his people:

And it is supposed to teach us how to change the way we think by learning how to deny or refuse ungodliness and worldly lusts (that we used to [as many still do] hold dear and esteem precious); and that we should be alert (sober) in the things of YAH pertaining to living righteously (not self-righteously through knowledge alone) and godly (walking in the Light as he is the Light) **IN THIS PRESENT WORLD.**

Before we can take claim and look forward to that blessed hope and glorious appearing of our Messiah, in which we do also look to be changed and glorified in our mortal bodies, changing from a corruptible body into a incorruptible body in HIS coming and appearing (in its proper season).

**"Now this I say, brethren, that flesh and blood cannot inherit the kingdom of YAH; neither doth corruption inherit incorruption. Behold, I shew you a mystery; We shall not all sleep, but WE SHALL BE CHANGED.**

In a moment, in the twinkling of an eye, at the last trump: for the trumpet shall sound, and the dead shall be RAISED INCORRUPTIBLE, AND WE SHALL BE CHANGED.

**For this corruptible must put on incorruption, and this MORTAL must put on IMMORTALITY.**
**So when this corruptible shall have put on incorruption, and this mortal shall have put on immortality, then shall be brought to pass the saying that is written, Death is swallowed up in victory."** *1* Corinthians (Qorintiym) 15:50-54

Again as was noted earlier "A prepared people for a prepared place."

"Let not your heart be troubled: ye believe in YAH, believe also in me. In my Father's house are many mansions: if it were not so, I would have told you. **I GO TO PREPARE A PLACE FOR YOU.**

**And if I go and prepare a place for you, I will come again, and receive you unto myself; that where I am, there ye may be also."** John (Yahuchanon) 14:1-3

Notice the Messiah stated that "He goes to prepare a place for you," that where he is, we may be also. Now, if that final resting place is the place we call "the land of Israel" today, which the Scriptures metaphorically notes as being Sodom and Egypt,

Revelation (Chizayon) 11:8, then why did he say that he goes to prepare a place?

New Jerusalem is that "new earth" that's preparing to descend in its time. New Jerusalem in the book of Revelations is described as being "sinless," no more deaths, no more tears. (Revelations 21-22).

So, our sinless lifestyle that we strive to seek after will be rewarded by a sinless city crafted and adorned **WITHOUT HANDS** and made eternal to us by the Father.

And although the servants to our people will aid in constructing walls within the city (Isaiah (Yesha'yahu) 60:10-22) – during the 1000 year reign when we (the remnant) will return to our homeland on this present earth – our FINAL resting place is "NEW JERUSALEM – whose builder and maker is YAH. "A prepared people for a prepared place."

# The Remnant

As concluding from the previous section of readings, I would be amiss if I did not inform you that not all who claim to be of Israel is not all Israel; and I would be wrong if I did not enlighten you to the fact that only the elected (remnant) of Israel will experience that place called New Jerusalem.

If you observe with me the book of Revelations (Chizayon) 22:11-13, the chapter that talks so much about the new City of David (as others note it to be, "the original Garden of Eden"), and the awe and beauty of this incredible place, these following statements were ironically positioned in the midst:

"He that is unjust, let him be unjust still: and he which is filthy, let him be filthy still: and he that is righteous, let him be righteous still: and he that is holy, let him be holy still.

**And, behold, I come quickly; and my reward is with me, to give every man according as his work shall be."**

At the return of our Messiah, those who practice righteousness will be rewarded for their continual practice in righteousness; those who strived to live a set-apart life (holy) will be rewarded for such. However, at his coming, those who continued to live unjustly will be rewarded according to fruits that were manifested from their unjust deeds. The same with those who continued to live a filthy lifestyle at his coming.

The significance of this passage is, most Israelites are under the assumption that these statements are only applicable to the so-called heathen – the non-Hebraic Gentiles and surrounding nations.

Conversely, I would like to bring to your attention the meaning and definition of the word unjust found in that passage of Scripture.

Unjust (from *Strong's* [*G91*]) adikeo: which means: to actively do wrong (morally, socially, or physically) to be an offender, to have violated the laws in some way; wickedly.

> **G91 - *adikeō***
> **Outline of Biblical Usage:**
> I. absolutely
>   A. to act unjustly or wickedly, to sin,
>   B. to be a criminal, to have violated the laws in some way
>   C. to do wrong
>   D. to do hurt
> II. transitively
>   A. to do some wrong or sin in some respect
>   B. to wrong some one, act wickedly towards him
>   C. to hurt, damage, harm

So, let me ask this question. If a nation of people were never given laws to govern them (the righteous laws of YAH) then how could that nation of people consciously or knowingly offend or violated those laws wickedly (without prior knowledge or awareness)?

Although many nations will be held accountable by the MOST HIGH YAH for their abominable and wicked acts, it is "Israel" who will be held primarily responsible because of this:

You cannot truly have the ability to be unjust unless you have the means to be considered just. In other words, a man/woman must be granted the privilege to be measured as just, righteous, and set-apart (holy) in order to be regarded as unjust, unrighteous, and unholy.

Again, the apostle Paul noted this:

**"For I could wish that myself were accursed from Christ for my brethren, my kinsmen according to the flesh:"** Romans (Romaiym) 9:3

So, who are Paul's kinsmen according to the flesh? Let's continue reading…

**WHO ARE ISRAELITES; to whom (or to them) pertaineth the adoption, and the glory, and the covenants, and the giving of the law, and the service of YAH, and the promises…"** Romans (Romaiym) 9:4

Although there are many talking points in these passages, I would like simply to note that it was the Israelites who were given the law in order to make one just, righteous, and set-apart (holy) people, with the ability to offend the law, to be deemed unjust, unrighteous, and unholy.

So, Revelations (Chizayon) 22:11-13 is directly tied into those to whom the law was given, who will be judged according to their works whether they be just or unjust. The apostle Peter noted this same fact in another way:

**"For the time is come that judgment must begin at the house of YAH: and if it first begins at us, what shall the end be of them that obey not the gospel of YAH? And if the righteous scarcely be saved, where shall the ungodly and the sinner appear?"** 1 Peter (Kepha) 4:17-18 (KJV)

So, let's break this statement down. According to 1 Peter 1:1, this letter was written to the **12 tribes of Israel scattered abroad**, and Peter acknowledges that judgment must begin with those to whom the law was given: – those with the ability to live upright lives – the House of YAH or the "Children of Israel" – the chosen people of YAH.

Peter continues to note that if judgment begins with us (the Hebrews/Israelites) who obeyed the gospel (the good news of our Messiah) what shall be the end of those (Hebrews/Israelites) who obeyed NOT the gospel of YAH? Remember who this letter was written to and for, as well as understand the topic of discussion, which is "the whole Nation of Israel" – the House of YAH" will be the first to stand in judgment in the presence of YAH.

And this judgment is NOT only for Israelites in our time, but the entire house from its conception, back to those who were first given the law: from Adam to Noah to Abraham and Isaac; Hebrews then Jacob (Israel) and his descendants, as well as Moses; the children of Israel, Hebrew Israelites, and so forth and so on.

**"Awake, sword, against my shepherd, against the man who is close to me!" declares the Almighty YAH. "Strike the shepherd, and the sheep will be scattered, and I will turn my hand against the little ones."**

"In the whole land," declares YAH, two-thirds (2/3) will be struck down and perish; yet one-third (1/3) will be left in it. This third (1/3) I will put into the fire; I will refine them like silver and test them like gold."

**Then they will call on my name and I will answer them; I will say, 'They (the 1/3) are my people,' and they will say, that YAH is our Father.'** Zechariah (Zakaryahu) 13:7-9

This is known to many as **"the remnant of our people – Israel."** Two-thirds of us will be stuck down and perish while one-third of our people (those who are set apart) will YAH purify, refine with fire (the testing of our faith in resembling our Father YAH), and bring with him. Then after the purification process, YAH will acknowledge that these, those who have been refined and purified will HE recognize as **"MY PEOPLE".**

Notice YAH is not recognizing the two-thirds of our people who have been cut off and killed as his people, but the one-third (the remnant) whom HE refined and purified as his people.

Which brings me to one of the most misunderstood passages of Scripture, which goes like this:

**"Not as though the word of YAH hath taken none effect. For they are not all Israel, which are of Israel: Neither, because they are the seed of Abraham, are they all children: but, In Isaac shall thy seed be called."** Romans (Romaiym) 9:6-7 (KJV)

AGAIN, READ CAREFULLY:

**"Well then, has YAH failed to fulfill his promise to Israel? No, for not all who are born into the nation of Israel are truly members of YAH's people! Being descendants of Abraham doesn't make them truly Abraham's children."** Romans (Romaiym) 9:6-7 (NLT)

So far, every time I hear a teaching on this passage of Scripture, nearly 99% percent of the time, everyone who expounds on this set of verses immediately digs into the second half that talk about how "not being a descendant of Abraham (such as Ishmael, Esau, the sons of Katorah, etc.) doesn't make you a child/children of the promises of YAH, but in Isaac were the promises given too, then directly to Jacob.

But rarely is it addressed: "Not all who are born into the nation of Israel are truly members of YAH's people." And the one percent explanation that I do hear is stating that this passage is talking about false Edomite Israelites. Unfortunately, it is not.

Again, this passage comes directly after the passage that states:

**"For I could wish that myself were accursed from the Messiah for my brethren, my kinsmen according to the flesh: WHO ARE ISRAELITES."** Romans (Romaiym) 9:3-4

So, let's not mistake Edomites as Paul's kinsmen according to the flesh. These passages are regarding the direct descendants of Israel, not imposters.

So then, who is truly Israel? Israel will be the one-third (1/3) of the elected (according to the flesh) whom YAH will purify and bring with him as noted in Zechariah 13:7-9, and not the two-thirds of his people who will be destroyed.

Paul also gave us a better understanding of this when he noted:

"For you are not a true Jew (Judahite/Israelite) just because you were born of Jewish parents (solely according to the flesh) or because you have gone through the ceremony of circumcision.

**No, a true Jew (according to the flesh) is one whose heart is right with YAH. And true circumcision is not merely obeying the letter of**

the law; rather, it is a change of heart produced by the Spirit. And a person with a changed heart seeks praise from YAH, and not from people." Romans (Romaiym) 2:28-29

This scriptural text has absolutely nothing to do with someone being adopted into the Israelite family as a Spiritual Jew. Paul is just expressing that a true Hebrew Israelites are not simply those who are born through ancestral lineage, who practice certain components of the Law. But YAH's true people are those who are not only are born through ancestral lineage, but also those of the lineage whose hearts have been circumcised and made right with YAH, produced by the fruit of the Spirit who only seeks to please YAH and not mankind (or the flesh).

Again, the people in Zechariah 13, will profess after going through the purification process (the fire) and being refined will announce that **"YAH is our Father"**.

And now this Scripture passage will make more sense and give you a better understanding of this mystery:

**"Even so then at this present time also there is a remnant according to the election of grace."** Romans (Romaiym) 11:5

"For I would not, brethren, that ye should be ignorant of this MYSTERY, lest ye should be wise in your own conceits; that blindness in part is happened to Israel, until the fullness of the Gentiles be come in.

"And so ALL ISRAEL shall be saved: as it is written, There shall come out of Zion the Deliverer, and shall turn away ungodliness from Jacob:" Romans (Romaiym) 11:26-27

I have heard that many conclude from this passage that it doesn't matter what Israel does or how Israel lives, because in the end we will all be saved (restored). Unfortunately, the understanding of the word mystery was missed and if that's the first understanding you come to by reading this, then where does the **mystery part** come into play?

Similar to playing the game of Clue, you cannot link the murderer in the game until you first find the weapon, the location, and the person by a series of questions and information that aids you in eliminating all/any information that doesn't apply directly to the clue – that's a mystery. Without the process, mysteries will remain mysteries which oftentimes lead people to add their own interpretations into the meaning to fit their personal agendas.

So, who then are the ALL ISRAEL who will be saved? As mentioned previously, these are those who YAH himself considers *"MY PEOPLE"*, who are the one-third he will bring with him through the purification process.

Even Esdras in 8: 1; 3 in the (Apocrypha) came to this conclusion after a series of questions for/with the Most High as delivered by his messengers to Esdras:

"And he answered me saying, The MOST HIGH, hath made this world for many, but the world to come for few." There be many created, but few shall be saved."

To conclude "Only a remainder or remnant of Israel will be restored in that great and mighty day of HIS return." Will you be numbered amongst the two-thirds who will be destroyed or the one-third who will be saved (restored/salvaged) as the governmental heads and leaders of the world to come?

Here are other Scripture passages that shed light on the mystery of the few who will be the saved/restored of Israel. All these scriptural passages refer to the Entire Nation of Israel in context:

**"Not every one that saith unto me, Ruler, Ruler, shall enter into the kingdom of heaven; but he that doeth the will of my Father which is in heaven.**

Many will say to me in that day, Ruler, Ruler have we not prophesied in thy name? and in thy name have cast out devils? and in thy name done many wonderful works?

**"And then will I profess unto them, I never knew you: depart from me, ye that work iniquity."** Matthew (Mattithyahu) 7:21-23

"Woe unto you that desire the day of the Anointed One! to what end is it for you? the day of the Anointed One is DARKNESS, and not light."

**"As if a man did flee from a lion, and a bear met him; or went into the house, and leaned his hand on the wall, and a serpent bit him.**

"Shall not the day of the Anointed One be darkness, and not light? even very dark, and no brightness in it?" Amos (Amoc) 5:18-20

---

**"'In those days, 'says YAH, 'no sin will be found in Israel or in Judah, for I will forgive the REMNANT I preserved.'"** Jeremiah (Yirmeyahu) 50:20

"Then at LAST YAH of Heaven's Armies will himself be Israel's glorious crown. He will be the pride and joy of the REMNANT of his people. "Isaiah (Yesha'yahu) 28:5

---

**"'And concerning Israel,' Isaiah the prophet cried out, "'though the people of Israel are as numerous as the sand of the seashore, only a REMNANT will be saved (restored/salvaged).**

For YAH will carry out his sentence upon the earth (upon all the world) with finality.'" Romans (Romaiym) 9:27-28

"A remnant will return; yes, the remnant of Jacob (Israel – both kingdoms) will return to the Mighty YAH.

But though the people of Israel are as numerous as the sand of the seashore, only a remnant of them will return. The Mighty One has rightly decided to destroy his people." Isaiah (Yesha'yahu) 10:21-22

---

"I will preserve a remnant of the people of Israel, and of Judah to possess my land. Those I choose will inherit, and my servants will live there." Isaiah (Yesha'yahu) 65:9

"For a remnant of my people will spread out from Jerusalem, a group of survivors from Mount Zion. The passionate commitment of YAH of Heaven's Armies will make this happen!" Isaiah (Yesha'yahu) 37:32

---

"The Messiah went through the towns and villages, teaching as he went, always pressing on toward Jerusalem. Someone asked him, 'Teacher, will only a few be saved?'

He replied, 'Work hard to enter the narrow door to YAH's

Kingdom, for many will try to enter but will fail.

**When the master of the house has locked the door, it will be too late. You will stand outside knocking and pleading, "Master, open the door for us!" But he will reply, 'I don't know you or where you come from.**

Then you will say, 'But we ate and drank with you, and you taught in our streets. And he will reply, 'I tell you, I don't know you or where you come from. Get away from me, all you who do evil.'

**There will be weeping and gnashing of teeth, for you will see Abraham, Isaac, Jacob, and all the prophets in the Kingdom of YAH, but YOU will be thrown out."** Luke (Lucus) 13:22-28

May our Heavenly Father Abba YAH continue Barak (or bless) you and your family as we continue to desire to learn and understand – first and foremost, the sincere milk of his Word (for those who are young or new to this walk) as we grow in grace and in the knowledge of our Messiah, whereby we can partake of the strong meat of his expressions. 1 Peter (Kepha) 2:2; Hebrews (Ivriym) 5:13-14

May our Father YAH continue to add to our understanding as we patiently wait (as set-apart people) for his glorious return. We, as his people, must continue to humble ourselves, pray, seek his face, and turn from our wicked ways in order to hear from heaven and our sins be forgiven. This will (in-turn) restore us, once again, in favor with Abba Father then he (in return) will gaze upon us and be even more attentive to the voice of our prayers and supplications towards him.

Finally, brothers and sisters, in these last days; we will hear many voices telling us **"thus saith the Father"** or **"we have to do this or that"** and we must be very careful that we no longer be as immature children, tossed and blown about by every wind of new teaching or voice. We will not be influenced when people try to <u>trick us with lies so clever</u> **they sound like the truth**. Ephesians (Eph'siym) 4: 14

But as spoken to us in the book of I John (Yahuchanon) 4:1: do not believe everyone who claims to speak by the Spirit of YAH; we must test them to see if the spirit they have comes from YAH because there are MANY false prophets (who resemble the sheep) in this world.

And how do we test or try the spirits? Our Messiah warned us in the epistle of John (Yahuchanon) 6:63 that the **WORDS** spoken by HIM: they are Spirit and they are Life (changing). When people say "thus saith the Ruach" – first, it has to be -- line upon line, precept by precept mirroring the words of our Abba Father and/or our Messiah in the proper context spoken.

Then, it (the message) MUST already bear witness in our spirit by confirmation – if not, we MUST be patient and wait for the endorsement before moving in any lead direction. In addition, we must view and analyze the fruits (works and/or lifestyle of that said person) whether their labor consistently produces good or bad fruit.

Because our Messiah clearly tells us in the book of Matthew (Mattithyahu) 7:15-20: **"Beware of False Prophets"** knowing that a good tree CANNOT (consistently) bring forth evil fruit neither can a corrupt tree (consistently) bring forth good fruit; and by their fruits and/or works manifested ---is how we will be able to see who they really are; whether a true follower of YAH and his dear SON: our Messiah or whether they are just another false prophet (spokesmen or spokeswomen) in this world: whether heathen or Hebrew (by nature but not by spirit).

Shalom

## ABOUT THE AUTHOR

# MITCHELL D. EWING SR.

A Veteran and service member of the United Stated Navy, Mitchell D. Ewing Sr. in 1989, first accepted his calling as a servant of the Most High YAH (short version of the Hebrew name for the title GOD) at the age of 18. Shortly after receiving various ministerial training, he was commissioned as a leader to teach the message of the Messiah and traveled nationwide (During his religious expedition).

He has well over 28 years of experience in public speaking & teaching through various leadership seminar trainings; however, he holds his greatest value in the Enlightenment and Discovery of the True Hebrew People according to Deuteronomy 28: "the (so-called) Black & Negro Race – Semitic," where titles and past accomplishments are less meaningful.

Now, author of five thought-provoking books – which can be accessed and purchased via: enlightpub.wix.com/enlightenment

- The Emancipation of Tithing (2012)
- Restoring Spiritual Health (2014)
- Leaving Christianity (2016)
- Deuteronomy 28 (2017)
- Harden Not Your Hearts (2020)

More importantly, Mitchell D. Ewing Sr. serves as a loving husband to his wife Bridget and a caring father to his four children, Zaria, Zanetta, Zashanae, and Mitchell D. Jr.

Mitchell D. Ewing Sr. attended UMT in Arlington, Virginia, where he received his BA degree in Business Management, and his graduate degree from the University of Phoenix, where he earned his MBA in Business Management and Leadership. He, his wife and family has been a great inspiration to countless people throughout his life and continues to serve as a role model as he strives to encourage many through enlightenment.

THE FOLLOWING IMAGES & PICTURES ARE DEPICTIONS OF WHAT POSSIBLY SOME OF OUR ANCESTORS MAY HAVE LOOKED LIKE PRIOR TO THE INVASION OF THE GREEKS/ROMANS/INDO-EUROPEANS/HEATHENS AS NOTED:

"And laid open the book of the law, wherein the heathen has sought to paint the likeness of their images"

I Maccabees 3:48

# REFERENCES

- Strong's Hebrew Lexicon (KJV).

- "Leaving Christianity" by Mitchell D. Ewing & Casey Clark

- References Retrieved from https://www.blueletterbible.org//lang/lexicon/lexicon.cfm.Strongs

- "Deuteronomy 28" by Mitchell D. Ewing

- Promise. (n.d.). Retrieved April 17, 2016, from http://www.merriam webster.com/dictionary/promise

- "Restoring Spiritual Health" by Mitchell D. Ewing

- Strong's Greek Lexicon (KJV). Retrieved from https://www.blueletterbible.org//lang/Lexicon/Lexicon.cfm?Strong

- BibleGateway. (n.d.). Retrieved April 30, 2016, from http://www.biblegateway.com/

- Afro-Asiatic Language Family by Irene Thompson updated March 27, 2013 by Jon Phillips. Retrieved from www.aboutworldlanguages.com/afro-asiatic- language-family

- Afro-Asiatic languages: distribution of the Afro-Asiatic languages. [Map/Still]. In Britannica Online for Kids. Retrieved from http://kids.britannica.com/elementary/art-19263

- Yiddish Language and Culture. By Tracey R. Rich. Retrieved from http://www.jewfaq.org/yiddish.htm Copy Right dates 2004-2011

- Homan's Illustrated Bible Dictionary. (2003, pg 1696). By Holman Bible Publishers.

- Nelson's New Illustrated Bible Manners & Customs.(1999, pgs 358-376). By Howard F. Vos.

- J. D. Douglas/Merrill C. Tenney; The New International Dictionary of the Bible (1963). Grand Rapids, MI: Zondervan Publishing House

- Merrill F. Unger/William White, Jr.; Vine's Expository Dictionary of Biblical Words (1984/1985). Nashville: Thomas Nelson Publishers

- J. D. Douglas/Merrill C. Tenney; Zondervan Illustrated Bible Dictionary (Revised by Moises Silva) (2009). Grand Rapids, MI: Zondervan Publishing House

- Herbert Lockyer, Sr.; Nelson's Illustrated Bible Dictionary

(1978). Camden, N.J: Thomas Nelson Publishers

- Encyclopaedia Britannica (1974/1976); 15th edition: the Micorpaedia: Ready Reference and Index, Macropaedia: Knowledge in Depth, and Propaedia: Outline of Knowledge.

- Overlords Of Chaos; The Jewish Conspiracy Article. http://www.overlordsofchaos.com/html/origin_of_the_word_jew.html

- www.pininterest.com; black bible characters James C. Lewis, Photographer Black Bible

www.ingramcontent.com/pod-product-compliance
Lightning Source LLC
Chambersburg PA
CBHW070614100426
42744CB00006B/476